The Chopsticks Diet

The Chopsticks Diet

Japanese-inspired recipes
for easy weight-loss

Kimiko Barber

Photography by Jean Cazals

Kyle Books

This edition published in 2009 by
Kyle Books, an imprint of Kyle Cathie Limited
www.kylecathie.com

Distributed by National Book Network
4501 Forbes Blvd., Suite 200,
Lanham, MD20706
Phone: (301) 459 3366

ISBN: 978-1-904920-98-4

Library of Congress Control Number: 2008938051

10 9 8 7 6 5 4 3 2

Kimiko Barber is hereby identified as the author of this
work in accordance with section 77 of Copyright, Designs
& Patents Act 1988.

Design: Lisa Pettibone
Photography: Jean Cazals
Food stylist: Marie-Ange La Pierre
Props stylist: Wei Tang
Project editor: Sophie Allen
Americanizer: Liana Krissoff
Copy editor: Anna Hitchin
Proofreader: Stephanie Evans
Production: Sha Huxtable

Reproduction by Colourscan
Printed and bound in Singapore by Tien Wah Press

Acknowledgements

My foremost thanks go to Kyle Cathie for commissioning
me to do this book and for all her generous help and kind
encouragement along the way.

Thanks also to Ivan Mulcahy for his reassuring guidance.

Another big thanks to the entire team at Kyle Cathie; the
ever enthusiastic and cheerful Sophie Allen the editor, Wei
Tang, props stylist who must have sourced practically every
variety of chopsticks available in London, and the designer
Lisa Pettibone. It has also been huge fun to work with a
French photographer and food stylist team—my special
thanks to Jean Cazals for taking beautiful photographs and
Marie-Ange Lapierre for food styling.

The last but by no means least thanks to my husband,
Stephen.

Ceramics used on pages 81, 87, 98, 136, 141, 153 were
made by the author.

Contents

Introduction   6

Meal plans   9

Ingredients   10

Breakfast   16

One-bowl lunch   30

Lunch on-the-go   60

Salads   70

Soups   104

Light Suppers   130

Hunger Busters   158

Desserts   166

Index   174

Directory   176

Introduction

There is only one simple way to lose weight—eat less. We all know this already, so why do we find it difficult to put into practice or to maintain it for a long time? It is because many diet methods involve radical changes to what you can eat and often refer to pre-calculated calories and tables of indices. *The Chopsticks Diet* is straightforward: there are no calorie counts and no tables, but it's full of easy, delicious, and healthy Japanese-inspired recipes to eat with chopsticks.

It is a myth that Japanese women don't get fat—there is no such thing as "slimmer genes" and women in Japan are just as concerned about weight as those of any other nationality. But Japanese women on the whole tend to be slimmer, keep their youthful appearance, and enjoy relatively healthy lifestyles for years longer than women in the West. Both Japanese men and women have the longest life expectancies in the world and suffer fewer cardiovascular diseases. Obesity, though, as the Western diet creeps into everyday life, is worryingly on the rise, if still considerably less than in other affluent industrialized nations. It is not what we are but what we eat, how we cook, and how we eat that determines our health and figure.

After having three children in my late thirties, I became and stayed comfortably middle-aged in shape and dressed in baggy clothes to hide my figure. Gone were fashionable skinny dresses and figure-conscious designer suits I loved wearing before, and my wardrobe became colonized by voluminous tent-like dresses, elasticated skirts and baggy trousers. A very poor excuse I know, but it was difficult to go on a diet while my children were small because I cooked separate meals for them, and feeding them often involved eating with them. Worst of all, I ended up picking their leftovers because I felt guilty for wasting food. I then had a grown-ups' dinner, often late in the evening with my husband. It was no wonder I put on weight and went up in dress size.

The essence of *The Chopsticks Diet* lies in the Japanese way of food—what they eat and how they eat—exemplified in chopsticks. Since Japanese food is to be eaten with chopsticks nearly all recipes in this book are designed for eating in this way. Many research findings suggest that eating with chopsticks slows people down and therefore they eat less. It is said that there is as much as a 20-minute time-lag between the stomach becoming full and telling the brain that you are full. Try eating the same amount of food with chopsticks as you would with a knife and fork and you will quickly realize that it is almost impossible. If you eat fast, as most of us do nowadays, your brain cannot accurately monitor the amount of food your stomach is receiving. So it is difficult to know when to stop, therefore we end up eating more than we need. Slow eating is good for you, especially if you want to lose weight.

And take a casual look at the size of portions served in Japanese restaurants and note how small they come. Japanese food is served and presented in small dishes—a diminutive rice or soup bowl sits comfortably in the palm, and small helpings of delicacies from land and sea are arranged in dainty little bowls and saucers—all perfectly designed for eating with chopsticks. There is a saying in Japanese—*hara hachibu*—which means literally that you should eat until you are about 80 percent satisfied and no more. Leave the table when you are still wishing to eat more but not when you are full.

Eating with chopsticks not only physically slows you down and encourages you to eat less, but it also has the psychological benefit of making you think about the food and the enjoyment you get from it. It naturally requires more concentration than eating with a knife and fork. I prefer using chopsticks, even for non-Japanese food, because it makes me feel more appreciative of food and to me it is a more elegant way of eating. It is interesting to see that today in Japan all school lunches are eaten with chopsticks instead of with an ugly utilitarian invention of the 1960s called a "spork" (a cross between a spoon and fork) that was intended to make the children eat their tasteless school meals as fast as possible. Japanese children nowadays (who have wonderful food prepared for them) are taught to use chopsticks with "grace" and to make elegant "chopstick strokes" because we believe that the correct use of chopsticks makes us appreciate food more and increases the pleasure of eating. Among the many foody proverbs in Japanese, "eat with the eyes" seems particularly relevant for explaining the ethos of *The Chopsticks Diet*. I used to think making food look more attractive was intended just for restaurants chefs, but the saying also applies to eating. It tells us to take a moment to look and contemplate, and above all, enjoy engaging all five senses of sound, scent, sight, touch and taste.

One of the significant factors that sets the Japanese way of eating apart and makes the nation healthy and slim is the high component of carbohydrate-based energy. In the Japanese diet, carbohydrates, mainly in the form of rice, make up a quarter of the total energy intake. In the West, however, carbohydrate is often portrayed as a villain for dieters and many diets demonize it. Research shows that the form of energy the body runs on, whether fats, sugar, or carbohydrates, makes no difference in losing weight. What matters is the quality of carbohydrate—whether it is "good" or "bad" carbohydrate. Good carbohydrate foods are those that are still in their natural state or are still similar to their natural state and not processed. Good carbohydrates are nutritious, and generally high in fiber, giving you more energy and keeping you feeling satisfied for a longer period of time. Fiber-rich foods also help to lower cholesterol levels as well as aiding the body to rid it of its toxins. Traditional Japanese meals feature many good carbohydrate foods such as fresh vegetables, rice, soba noodles, and beans—which all appear extensively in this book. And here is another significant factor that sets Japanese food apart and makes it so healthy and slimming—we don't add fat to our carbohydrates. Rice is delicious to eat on its own and doesn't need additions of fat or sugar like butter or sweet jams. Noodles are cooked in water and eaten with non-fat dashi-based dipping sauce with vegetables. Both rice and soba noodles are less processed than breads and pasta. Many recipes in the book also feature a number of diet-friendly fiber-rich ingredients such as agar-agar, bamboo shoots, burdock, konnyaku, seaweeds, and high-vitamin green tea.

There is also no tradition of roasting a large piece of meat in Japanese cooking, indeed many households in Japan still do not have an oven but cook with surface-heat. This is because meat and poultry were forbidden up until the mid-nineteenth century. So this book is full of salads and food that is gently steamed, simmered in flavorsome dashi, broiled, or stir-fried using little oil.

But the Japanese are eating more Westernized and processed food today than ever before and that is taking its toll on the nation's health. The most striking example is seen in the islands of Okinawa—the archipelago in the South-China Sea, once considered a Shangri-La on the sea, where septuagenarians were regarded mere babies, men and women in their 80s and 90s grew vegetables in their gardens and centenarians were no big deal. Okinawa became the largest American military base in Japan after the end of the Second World War. It took only a few decades to create a different health profile of this one-time health paradise. Okinawans in their 40s and below have grown up on a standard American diet of animal protein, especially red meat and highly processed food such as hamburgers, deep-fried potatoes, and bread instead of the traditional Okinawan diet of rice, home-grown vegetables, and fresh seafood and seaweeds. The health statistics of these younger Okinawans are alarming. Today this Okinawan age group has higher rates of obesity, and a greater risk of cardiovascular disease, liver disease, and premature death than the overall Japanese population.

The Chopsticks Diet was conceived while I was writing two Japanese cookbooks back-to-back. I ate the food I tested for the books with chopsticks. I am not expecting you to eat Japanese food with chopsticks every day for every meal, but I do suggest taking the concept of the book into consideration. Try eating Japanese-inspired food with chopsticks as often as you can—this will be easier to do at home but may be difficult when you eat out. I was so impressed when I once witnessed an Englishman whipping a pair of chopsticks out of his suit pocket in the middle of a very smart restaurant in London to eat mushroom risotto and arugula salad. A classic case of English eccentricity maybe, but when you are eating out in a restaurant or at a friend's house, try emulating chopstick eating—choose less processed food and order more Japanese-like dishes of vegetables and fish and preferably less red meat if possible. In the absence of chopsticks, use a knife and fork with *The Chopsticks Diet* in mind and slow down, cut the food into small pieces, put the knife and fork down between each mouthful and take time to chew and savor the food. You will enjoy the food more that way and the person who has cooked it will be pleased with the care and attention you are paying to their cooking.

Of course eating less food alone does not make you lose weight automatically. Food input is only one side of the equation and you must raise the level of energy output if you want to lose weight. *The Chopsticks Diet* is to help you to eat less and eat healthily, while it is you alone who can control your output of energy, by exercising regularly and maintaining your health and well-being. Exercising regularly is paramount for keeping fit and shedding weight safely. You will find that the more you eat well the better you feel and the more you enjoy exercise. It is a great cycle of joy in life.

A nice glass of wine adds pleasure to a meal and I am certainly not preaching to you to give up alcohol even while you are trying to lose weight. But if you are wondering why that five pounds is refusing to leave you despite healthy and sensible eating and regular exercise—the answer probably lies in your alcohol consumption. Alcohol is second only to fat in the amount of calories it provides but they are "empty" calories—they won't give you sustainable energy or fill you up. A typical glass of white wine (120ml/^{1}/$_2$ cup) amounts to 77 calories and 80 calories for red wine that is roughly an equivalent to a sweaty 10-minute session on a crossbar trainer in the gym. So my advice is to consume in moderation.

This is a book about the Japanese way of food and about discovering the joy and pleasure of delicious and easy Japanese-inspired home cooking and eating. I am certain that *The Chopsticks Diet* will help you to feel and look fantastic.

Here are some suggestions for what to eat for your three meals a day through the seasons.

Spring meal plan
- Japanese rice porridge (p19)
- Asparagus & anchovy domburi (p31) or Omusubi (rice balls) (p67) or Tofu salad (p82)
- Clam chowder miso soup with crisp deep-fried tofu (p126) or Bamboo shoot sushi (p133)

Summer meal plan
- Steamed green tea & blueberry muffins (p22) or a smoothie (p26)
- Zucchini & tomato domburi (p32) or Chilled soba noodles with gazpacho sauce (p52) or any salads and why not try Baked eggplant with grated daikon on green tea soba noodles (p49)
- Classic salmon sashimi with daikon salad (p86) or Beef carpaccio & eggplant with ginger dressing (p100) or Chilled misopacho (p110) with any salads

Summer picnic
- Tofu Spanish omelet (p25), Rolled sushi (p62) to impress your friends or Fresh spring rolls (p68) and don't forget to take some salads

Autumn meal plan
- Swirled egg brown rice porridge (p21) or Tofu Spanish omelet (p25)
- Chile mushrooms & tofu domburi (p34) or Spiced lentils with shrimp (p38) or try Nori & arugula soba in broth (p50) or Japanese mushrooms with soba noodles in green tea broth (p51)
- Japanese mushroom miso soup (p113) or Creamy roast pumpkin miso soup (p114) or Sea bream on rice (p147)

Winter meal plan
- Adzuki & rice porridge (p20)
- Warm lentils with tofu & spinach (p40) or Crisp duck with orange & watercress salad (p103)
- Okonomiyaki (p122) or Country-style kayu with chicken (p140) or Salmon hotpot (p152)

Ingredients

People tell me that the greatest barrier to learning Japanese cooking is not so much the cooking techniques, but the ingredients. Faced with unfamiliar foods, even the most adventurous cook may be perplexed in a Japanese food store. The purpose of this section is to provide a simple and helpful guide to some Japanese ingredients that are used in this book. Included are notes about storage and how long foods will keep.

Adzuki (azuki) beans

This small red bean is the second most frequently used legume in Japanese cooking, after the soybean. Dried adzuki beans that need soaking and cooking are widely available in supermarkets and health-food shops. The ready-to-use canned variety is also becoming easier to find in larger supermarkets. Store in a dry pantry.

Daikon (Japanese giant white radish)

Daikon (see top left opposite page) is aptly written as "big root" in Japanese. A typical daikon grows about 14 inches long, and as thick as a large zucchini. Daikon is one of the most important ingredients in Japanese cooking and is easy to find in most Asian grocery stores. Choose one that feels solid, has tight skin, and is free from bruises. Keep refrigerated.

Daikon is also available in other forms. Pickled daikon—takuan—is bright yellow, crunchy, and pungent. Dried and shredded daikon is called kiriboshi daikon and needs to be soaked before cooking.

Gobou (burdock)

This long, thin root vegetable has long been used by the Chinese in their herbal medicine; only the Japanese eat it. Covered in a dark brown skin, it can measure as much as 50 inches in length but is usually about 18 inches long. The skin has the most flavor, so it is best to scrub it clean and not peel it. It must be submerged in cold water as soon as it is cut to stop discoloring and take away any bitterness. Fresh burdock is available all year round from Japanese food stores. Frozen pre-shaved burdock is also sold in bags in Japanese food stores.

Goma (sesame seeds)

Both white and black sesame seeds are used in Japanese cooking, either in whole or ground form. The taste and aroma of sesame seeds intensify when heated or ground. Ready-toasted sesame seeds are available from Japanese food stores. Store in lidded jars in a dry kitchen cupboard.

Hijiki (hijiki seaweed)

Hijiki is a twiggy, olive-brown marine plant that grows to 12–40 inches in height. In Japanese food or health stores, it is nearly always sold in dried form. Dried hijiki must be soaked in water to reconstitute before use. It expands to ten times its volume when softened. Store in a dark, dry kitchen cupboard.

Kanten (agar agar)

Agar agar (see top right opposite page) is a pure form of vegetarian gelatin which is made of red seaweed, called tengusa ("heavenly grass") in Japanese. It comes in three forms: bar, filament, and powder. Outside Japan, you are most likely to find the powder form conveniently packed in 4g sachets that can be used like conventional gelatin powder. Compared to animal gelatin, agar agar sets more quickly, is more heat tolerant, and, above all, completely free of smell or taste and lacks the rubberiness of gelatin. Keep in a dark, dry kitchen cupboard for up to 6 months.

Katsuo-bushi (bonito fish flakes)

The bonito, a member of the mackerel family, has been an important ingredient in Japanese cooking both as a

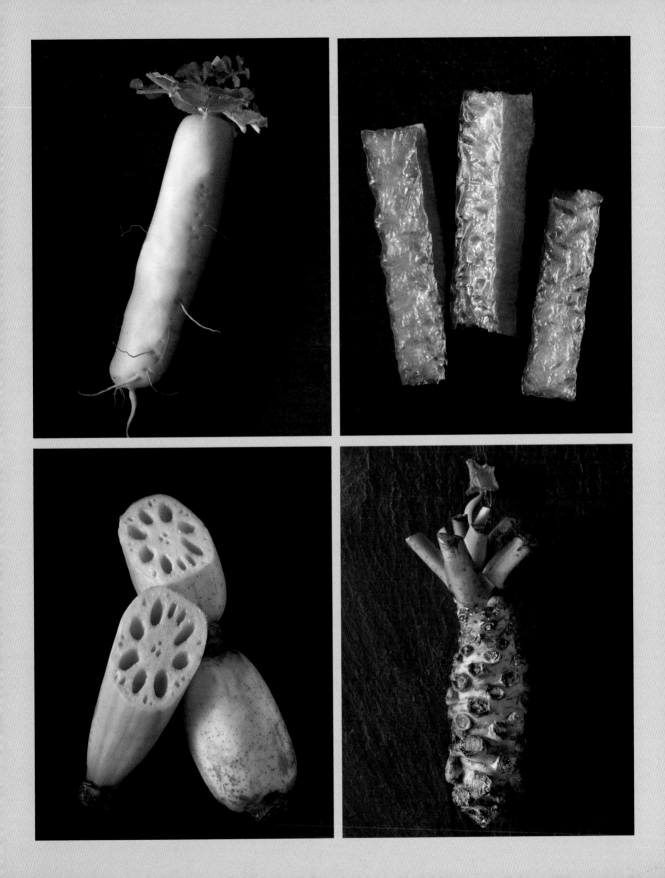

food and a seasoning ingredient. Fish flakes (see top left opposite page) are made by shaving the dried and smoked fish fillet. The flakes look like pale rose-colored wood shavings and have a distinct smoky aroma and taste. They are sold in cellophane packs of various sizes—from handy 4g single-use packets to more economical larger bags. If stored in a dark dry kitchen cupboard, flakes will keep for up to 12 months, but use within 3 months once the seal is opened.

Kome (rice)

Nearly half of the world's population depends on rice, and in Japanese, the word "gohan" means both "a meal" and "cooked rice." In other words, for the Japanese, a bowl of rice is a meal in itself; they are inseparable and it is almost impossible to talk about Japanese food without talking about rice. Highly polished white rice has always been at the top of the Japanese food hierarchy. The economic boom of the 1980s affected every aspect of life in Japan, including food, and the result was that the more exotic, expensive, and sometimes downright extravagant a food was, the more eagerly it was sought after. Even rice had to be a "designer" or "brand" food and became ever more processed. The excess did not last long, and after the bubble burst, there followed over a decade in the economic doldrums. Japanese people returned to their previous way of eating, enjoying simple, frugal, and more wholesome food. They didn't have to look very far but had only to embrace many of their traditional foods such as home-grown vegetables and seasonings such as miso, and, above all, rice. The rice they now enjoyed was the rice once thought to be old-fashioned, unsophisticated, unpolished, or half-polished: brown rice.

Brown rice is the most important source of energy in the Japanese diet. It is unmilled, leaving the bran, germ, and aleurone layers intact. These nutrients occur mainly in the rice "embryo," which is removed from processed rice as it is polished. Brown rice takes two to three times longer to cook and has a chewy texture. It is harder to digest and therefore sustains you for much longer. Brown rice also requires more chewing—a good habit to get into since it produces more saliva to aid digestion. The additional chewing slows down consumption.

There is a halfway compromise called "haiga seimai," which is a part-polished rice. The embryo is still intact and therefore contains about twice the amount of vitamins and minerals as white rice. But it cooks more quickly than brown rice. Although all Japanese grocers stock it, it is hard to distinguish from the ordinary, polished white rice since it is simply translated into English as "rice." My advice is to ask for help.

Konbu (kelp seaweed)

Konbu is one of the two basic ingredients for making dashi (Japanese stock), on which numerous Japanese dishes depend. There are many varieties, and it is cultivated mainly in the cold waters off the northern-most island of Hokkaido. The typical deep olive-brown kelp leaf grows 8 inches wide and 11 yards long. Konbu is sold dried and cut into manageable lengths. Choose dark and thick ones and store in a dark dry kitchen cupboard for up to 12 months.

Konnyaku (devil's tongue)

Konnyaku gel (top right opposite page) must rank at the top of the list of Japan's strange foods. The root of this plant is made into flour and compressed into a slab. Although there are many varieties of color and shape, standard konnyaku sold in Japanese food stores in the West is gray with dark speckles, in blocks 6 x 2½ inches and about ½ inches thick. It is normally sold vacuum-packed with a little limewater. Store in a dark kitchen cupboard for up to 3 months but once opened, refrigerate in a clean bowl of water. Change the water daily and use within 2 weeks. All konnyaku should be boiled briefly before use.

Mirin (sweet cooking sake)

This sweetened cooking sake looks like a thin golden syrup and has a round, mild alcoholic aroma. It is used in cooking to add a sweet taste and to create a glossy appearance. Mirin is sold in bottles of various sizes. Store in a cool place, away from direct sunlight. Once the seal is broken, the aroma will begin to deteriorate and it should be kept refrigerated.

Miso (fermented soybean paste)

Miso (bottom left opposite page) is one of the most important staples in Japanese cooking. There are numerous varieties, each with its own taste, aroma, color, and texture. The color is generally a good guide to taste and texture—the lighter the color, the less salty the flavor and the softer the texture. They are all made by essentially the same method: crushed, boiled soybeans, on their own or often with rice, wheat, or barley, are left to ferment and mature for months or even up to 3 years. In this book, I often recommend using more than one variety to create more interesting tastes so it might be helpful to buy small quantities of different types. Japanese food stores carry nearly a dozen different kinds of miso, and health-food stores often have at least half a dozen types. If refrigerated, miso will keep for up to 12 months in airtight containers.

Nori (laver seaweed)

Today nearly all nori is farmed. Spores are planted on nets placed in sheltered shallow bays in January and harvested in the autumn. Mature plants are gathered, washed in fresh water, and laid in thin sheets to dry like handmade paper and then toasted. A sheet of dry, toasted nori comes in a standard size of 7 x 8 inches and is sold in bundles of ten. The price is a good indication of the quality; also, choose thick, glossy, dark olive-brown sheets. Nori also comes ready-shredded or seasoned. It should be stored in a dark, dry kitchen cupboard and once opened, nori should be kept in airtight plastic bags and used as soon as possible. If nori becomes limp, toast it over a gentle flame to revive the aroma and crispness before use.

Rencon (lotus root)

Lotus root (bottom left page 11) is actually a buff-colored rhizome, typically measuring nearly 1 yard long and 2 1/2 inches thick. It is divided into cylinder-like segments, each up to 6 inches. Air passages run through the length of the rhizome, which give it an attractive appearance in cross-section like a paper-chain. Although fresh lotus roots are becoming more readily available from Asian and Japanese food stores outside the country, you are most likely to come across the "fresh boiled" variety vacuum packed with a little water or in cans. Fresh lotus roots should be stored in a cool, dark place in the same way as potatoes, although they do not keep as long.

Sake

Sake, dashi, soy sauce, miso, and rice vinegar are the "big five" in Japanese cooking. In nearly every Japanese dish, one or more of these ingredients is used. In cooking, sake is used to tenderize and to suppress saltiness; it also helps to eliminate fishy tastes and smells and to revive the delicate tastes of other ingredients. Although cheaper cooking sake is available, personally I do not recommend it, as it tends to have an inferior flavor and aroma. Besides, only a small amount is used in cooking. Sake is sold in bottles or cartons in various quantities in liquor stores, supermarkets, and Japanese food stores. Once the seal is opened, keep it in a cool, dark kitchen cupboard and use within 3 months.

Shoyu (soy sauce)

Soy sauce is indisputably one of the five most important ingredients in Japanese cooking. It is made from fermented soybeans, water, salt, and wheat. It has a beautiful spectrum of colors, ranging from warm amber and deep brown to shimmering purple. It also carries complex aromas. The fermentation of soybeans converts its protein into amino acids and the carbohydrate of the wheat into glucose that together give the distinct, appetizing taste of soy sauce. Outside Japan, cooks are likely to find three types of soy sauce: an all-purpose dark soy; a saltier, light soy; and the wheat-free and slightly thicker tamari. Buy small quantities, refrigerate after opening, and use within a few months.

Soba (buckwheat noodles)

Soba noodles are made from buckwheat flour. Buckwheat is a fast-growing, hardy annual plant native to central Asia and China. It has long been eaten in Japan, first as a cereal, in a dumpling form, and much later as noodles. It is difficult to make noodles exclusively from buckwheat flour as the buckwheat proteins are completely gluten-free and therefore do not bind easily into a noodle shape. So most soba noodles contain some wheat or mountain yam, or both, as binding agents. When cooking the noodles, a glass of cold water is poured into the saucepan of boiling water to ensure that the inner core of each noodle strand is cooked at the same rate as the outside.

Su (vinegar)

Japanese rice vinegar has a much milder strength than most Western vinegars. The manufacturing process is a cross between that of sake and soy sauce. The rice is washed, soaked, and steamed, and then yeast is added to form a rice culture that converts sake-like alcohol into vinegar. Most Japanese rice vinegars range in color from pale golden to light bronze and have pleasant and mild yet astringent tastes and aromas. It is sold in bottles of different quantities in Japanese food stores and larger supermarkets. Store in a cool, dark cupboard. Once opened, use within 6 months.

Takenoko (bamboo shoots)

Freshly dug bamboo shoots in their husks are the first sign of spring in Japan. In the West, bamboo shoots are available ready-cooked in cans from Asian food stores and larger supermarkets. Freshly-cooked shoots, vacuum-packed in water, are sold all year round in Japanese food stores. Wash thoroughly and remove the grainy white residue, a result of the commercial preparation process, which has an unpleasant sour taste. Both canned and water-packed bamboo shoots will keep for about a week if refrigerated in clean water. Change the water every day.

Tea

There are many varieties of green tea, but for the purpose of this book, I use the ceremonial matcha, or green tea powder, and all-purpose sencha. Matcha is made from freshly picked young leaves that are steamed, dried, and ground to a powder. It can be expensive and is sold in small quantities. Like ordinary tea leaves, matcha and sencha should be stored in a dry cupboard away from direct sunlight.

Tofu

Tofu is soybean curd made from coagulated soymilk. Soybeans are soaked overnight, boiled, ground, and strained. A coagulant—magnesium chloride—is added to form a curd in a muslin-lined mold. Firm tofu is slightly off-white and firm enough to handle, while soft silken tofu is pure white and more delicate. Fresh tofu is normally sold in a plastic container filled with a little water. Tofu is essentially a fresh food and should be used within a few days. Keep refrigerated in fresh water.

Deep-fried tofu is often sold frozen. Once defrosted, it should be used within a few days.

Umeboshi (pickled plum)

Umeboshi (bottom right page 12) is made from unripe green plums, soaked in brine, packed with red perilla leaves, and left to pickle. It is sold in Japanese food stores or health-food stores in jars or plastic tubs. Once opened, it keeps almost indefinitely, if refrigerated.

Wakame (soft seaweed)

Wakame is a member of the brown algae family. In Japanese food stores, larger supermarkets, and health-food stores outside Japan, wakame is nearly always sold in a dried form. Before use, dried wakame must be soaked in water. Store in a dark, dry kitchen cupboard.

Wasabi (Japanese green horseradish)

Wasabi (bottom right page 11) is written as "mountain hollyhock" in Japanese and is one of the strongest spices used in Japanese cooking. Its natural habitat is the marshy edge of cold, clear mountain streams. Today nearly all fresh wasabi sold is cultivated in remote flooded mountain terraces. The root part of this perennial aquatic plant typically grows to the size of an average carrot, but it is green and knobbly. Although many high-quality Japanese restaurants serve freshly grated wasabi, most home cooks in the West are likely to encounter wasabi either in powder form or as a ready-mixed paste in a small plastic tube. Both powder and tube wasabi are sold in Japanese food stores or larger food stores. Treat the wasabi powder in the same way as mustard powder and keep it in a dark, dry kitchen cupboard. Wasabi paste needs to be refrigerated after opening and used within a few months.

Yuzu (Japanese citron)

The yuzu fruit is bright yellow and about the same size as a tangerine. The fruit is used purely for its marvellous aromatic rind and fragrant juices. In the West, fresh yuzu is difficult to find, but the juice is sold in small bottles in Japanese food stores. Bottled yuzu juice is expensive, but a little goes a long way. Keep refrigerated and shake well before use.

The traditional Japanese breakfast consists of a bowl of freshly cooked rice or rice porridge, a bowl of hot miso soup with tofu or wakame seaweed, a plate of grilled fish, simmered seasonal vegetables, and an egg dish such as a rolled omelet, accompanied by side dishes such as a small helping of natto (sticky fermented soybeans), a tiny dish of seasoned seaweed, or a few sheets of dried seasoned nori, and an assortment of pickled vegetables. It is a pretty long menu to prepare first thing in the morning and, to be honest, I doubt if many households in Japan today feature such an elaborate and labor-intensive fare every morning. Japanese people today reserve such a big breakfast tray for weekends or for when they are staying at an inn or a hotel on vacation. The everyday average Japanese breakfast is a much more simplified version of the menu above, although rice and miso soup always appear.

The Japanese love breakfast. The nation that has longer life spans than any other and enjoys relatively good health knows the importance of a good breakfast. Do not skip breakfast—it is the most important meal of the day. Skipping breakfast will cause your blood sugar level to drop so low that by mid-morning your brain is unable to concentrate, your tummy is rumbling, and you will be tempted to reach out for a quick sugar fix such as a bar of chocolate. In an ideal world, I would feast like an emperor in the morning, eat like a queen at lunchtime, and like a pauper in the evening. I think we all really know the importance of breakfast and the harm caused by skipping it, but none of us lives in an ideal world and we all seem to be rushing out the door in the morning. This is why I have included a small number of delicious Japanese-inspired breakfast recipes that are all "doable" to get you started.

Breakfast

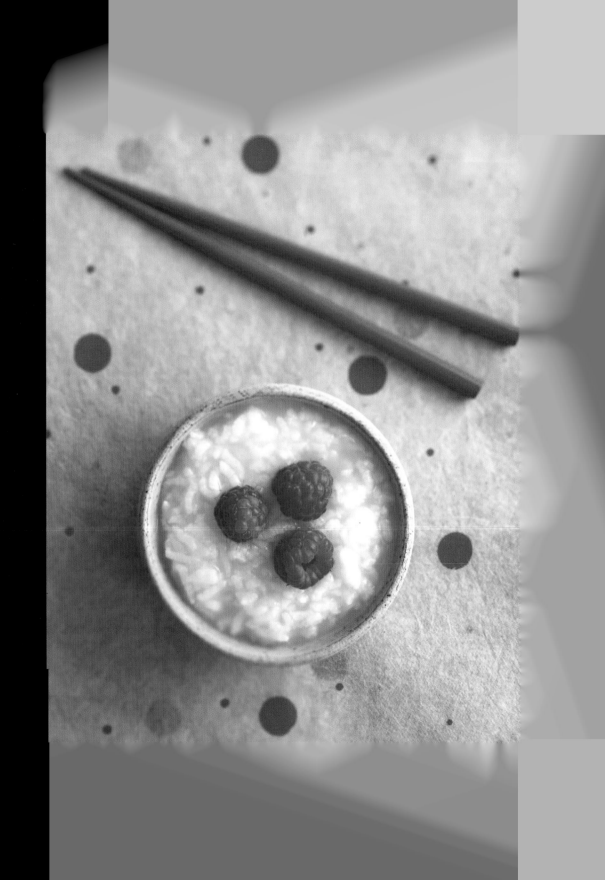

Japanese rice porridge

Serves 2

- ¼ cup Japanese-style short-grain rice
- 1½ cups water
- ¼ teaspoon salt
- a handful of raspberries

An eminent thirteenth-century Zen Buddhist monk, Dohgen, wrote that there are ten benefits to enjoy from a bowl of "kayu," Japanese rice porridge: it gives glossy and healthy skin, strengthens the body and soul, promotes longevity, is easy to digest and good for the brain, helps to maintain warmth, staves off hunger, quenches thirst, and promotes healthy bowel movements. This all sounds excellent, if not almost too good to be true, considering it is only a humble bowl of soupy rice!

There is a varying degree of consistency in Japanese rice porridge, depending on the amount of water. In this recipe, the rice is cooked with six times as much of water, which makes the porridge quite soupy and light but still sustaining.

Put the rice in a sieve and wash it under cool, running water until the rinsing water becomes clear. Ideally, washing the rice should be done at least half an hour before cooking to let the rice absorb the moisture and plump up. This can also be done the night before.

However, if you forget and are short of time, put the washed rice in a saucepan with the measured amount of water and let it sit for 10 minutes before turning the heat on. The ideal saucepan is heavy-based with a tight-fitting lid. Put on the lid and bring the rice to boil over a high heat—this should take about 5 minutes. Move the lid slightly and reduce the heat to low and allow to simmer for 20–25 minutes.

Turn off the heat, season with the salt, replace the lid, and let it steam for 5 minutes. Serve with the raspberries in warmed bowls with chopsticks.

Tip
Instead of raspberries, try this with the traditional accompaniment of umeboshi (pickled plums).

Adzuki & rice porridge

Serves 2

- 2 tablespoons dried adzuki beans, soaked in water overnight
- 2^1/$_2$ cups water
- ^{1}/$_4$ cup Japanese-style short-grain rice, washed and then drained for 30 minutes

Adzuki beans have long been associated with auspiciousness in Japan. According to custom, adzuki porridge is eaten on January 15 to celebrate the Little New Year on the old lunar calendar. Indeed, no celebration feast is complete without adzuki rice. The main components of adzuki beans are glucose and protein, but their rich vitamin B1, potassium, and highly edible fiber help to lower blood pressure, overcome fatigue, and reduce swellings. Together, its gentle, sweet taste and warm pink appearance make this porridge a cheerful breakfast.

Put the adzuki beans in a heavy-bottom saucepan (do not use a cast-iron pan as the iron reacts and will discolor the beans). Add the measured amount of water and cook over medium heat until the beans become tender—this should take about 30–40 minutes. Top up with boiling water if necessary. Save the cooking liquid and measure it to 2 cups.

Put the rice and adzuki cooking liquid in a heavy-bottom saucepan with a lid and bring to a boil over a high heat. Remove the lid to prevent it from boiling over. Reduce the heat to low to simmer for 20 minutes longer. Turn off the heat and replace the lid, allowing it to steam for 5 minutes. Serve hot in warmed bowls with chopsticks.

Tip
Because adzuki beans require long and slow cooking, I recommend cooking a large quantity and then keeping them refrigerated in the cooking liquid for up to a week.

Swirled egg brown rice porridge

Brown rice is much healthier than polished white rice and should become a staple in your diet. It needs one third more water to cook than polished white rice and takes a little longer to cook. It also requires much more chewing to get the full benefits and this is good news, especially for dieters, because brown rice will keep you feeling satisfied much longer.

Start by soaking the rice with the measured amount of water in a heavy-bottom saucepan overnight. Place a tight-fitting lid on the saucepan and bring to a boil over medium heat, then reduce the heat slightly and cook for 40–45 minutes longer.

Add the beaten eggs, stir to swirl, and season with the soy sauce. Garnish with scallions and nori. Serve with chopsticks.

Tip
Cooking with a pressure cooker will halve the preparation time.

Serves 2

- $1/4$ cup brown rice, soaked in water overnight
- $2 1/2$ cups water
- 2 eggs, lightly beaten
- 1 tablespoon soy sauce
- 2 scallions, finely chopped
- a handful of shredded nori

Steamed green tea & blueberry muffins

Makes 6 regular muffins

- 6 tablespoons plus 1 teaspoon superfine sugar
- $1/3$ cup water
- 1 egg, lightly beaten
- 1 tablespoon vegetable oil
- $1^2/3$ cups whole-wheat flour
- 2 teaspoons baking powder
- 1 teaspoon matcha (green tea powder) plus extra for garnish
- $1/3$ cup fresh blueberries

This recipe is so simple that you can easily make these delicious muffins for breakfast. If well wrapped, the muffins will keep for 3 days so they are brilliant for breakfast on the run.

Put the sugar and water in a saucepan and bring to a boil while stirring to dissolve all the sugar and set aside to cool.

Put the egg in a bowl, add the sugar water, and whisk to mix well. Gradually add the oil into the mixture and sift in the flour, baking powder, and tea. Fold in the blueberries.

Spoon the mixture into a lightly greased muffin tin or muffin cases. Place the tin in a rapidly boiling steamer and steam for 15 minutes. (If the muffin tin doesn't fit place the muffins into muffin cases and steam in batches.)

Sprinkle with a little extra matcha to serve.

Tofu Spanish omelet

Serves 2

- ¼ (12-ounce) package soft silken tofu
- 1 teaspoon vegetable oil
- 3 eggs, lightly beaten
- 1 tablespoon light soy sauce
- 1 medium tomato, deseeded and roughly chopped
- 2 scallions, roughly chopped

This adaptation of the rustic Spanish recipe uses tofu instead of potatoes, which makes it a real "power breakfast" that is easy to digest.

Drain the tofu by wrapping it in a piece of paper towel and microwaving it for 30 seconds on medium-high. Cut into ¾-inch cubes.

Heat the oil in a small omelet pan over medium heat. Mix the eggs and the soy sauce and add to the pan to cook for 2–3 minutes or until the outer edge becomes set but the omelet is still runny in the center.

Add the tofu, tomato, and scallions to cook for 2 minutes longer. To turn over the omelet, take the pan off the heat, slide the omelet onto a dinner plate, invert the pan over the omelet, and turn over both the plate and the pan.

Return the pan to the heat to cook for 3–4 minutes or until the underside is cooked. Transfer the omelet to a cutting board, cut it into bite-size wedges, and serve.

Japanese rolled omelet with nori

Serves 2

- 3 eggs
- 1 tablespoon mirin
- 2 teaspoons light soy sauce
- ½ teaspoon vegetable oil
- 2 sheets of nori, torn into small pieces

You need a small nonstick omelet pan for this recipe.

Put the eggs, mirin, and soy sauce in a small bowl and beat lightly to mix. Heat the omelet pan over medium heat and brush with the oil. Pour in a third of the egg mixture and when the surface begins to dry, add a third of the torn nori pieces to roughly cover the egg.

Gather the omelet towards you and pour in another third of the egg mixture. Repeat the cooking process until you have used all the egg mixture and nori.

Transfer the omelet to a cutting board, roll tightly, and cut into bite-size pieces, and serve with chopsticks.

Smoothies

Serves 2

Pictured are:
Green Tea and Tofu Smoothie and
Tofu and Stawberry Smoothie

Tofu & apple smoothie

- $1/4$ (12-ounce) package soft silken tofu
- 2 apples, peeled, cored, and roughly chopped
- 1 cup apple juice
- 2 tablespoons runny honey
- 1 inch fresh ginger, peeled and roughly chopped

Put all the ingredients in a blender or food processor, and blend until smooth.

Tofu & strawberry smoothie

- $1/4$ (12-ounce) package soft silken tofu
- $3/4$ cup strawberries, hulled
- 1 cup soymilk
- 2 tablespoons runny honey

Put all the ingredients in a blender or food processor, and blend until smooth.

Green tea & tofu smoothie

- $1/4$ (12-ounce) package soft silken tofu
- 1 cup soymilk
- 1 teaspoon matcha (green tea powder)
- 1 tablespoon kinako (soybean flour)
- 1 tablespoon soft dark brown sugar

Put all the ingredients in a blender or food processor, and blend until smooth.

Green tea milkshake

- 2 bananas, roughly chopped
- 1 kiwi fruit, roughly chopped
- 1 cup soymilk
- 1 teaspoon matcha (green tea powder)
- 1 tablespoon runny honey

Put all the ingredients in a blender or food processor, and blend until smooth.

Lunch in the Japanese culinary history became established sometime around the seventeenth century when food productions especially rice increased. After breakfast, lunch is the second most important meal of the day, especially for those watching their weight, as there are still many hours left to burn off the food before bedtime. Based on their health benefits, I have selected two major sources of energy—rice and soba noodles—and designed the recipes around them. Both are delicious, healthy and nourishing and do not make you feel bloated or sleepy and are guaranteed to leave you feeling satisfied for many guilt-free hours afterwards. The two are easy and quick to prepare and can be eaten either hot or cold and lend themselves to microwave reheating if you want to take them to work. Soba noodles are made of buckwheat flour, which is completely gluten free, rich in edible fiber, and contains vitamin P that not only helps to lower cholesterols and is an antioxidant but recent researches show it helps to prevent accumulation of body fat—what more could you ask for!

Domburi is the generic term for all-in-one-bowl rice food, typically served to busy people at lunch times. Traditional toppings such as chicken and egg, or sautéd beef and onion, or grilled eel are served on top of rice in a big ceramic bowl with a lid. I have applied the basic concept of domburi to create delicious and healthy one-course lunches. The domburi concept is also versatile and practical— leftovers from previous evening meals are easily adaptable to make domburi toppings. So there is no excuse for having an unhealthy lunch!.

One-bowl lunches

How to cook brown rice

Brown rice is 74–77 percent carbohydrate and 6 percent protein (the remaining 20 percent is water, fiber, oil, vitamins, and minerals). It is the single most important source of energy in the Japanese diet. Compared to white rice, it contains four times the edible fiber, vitamins B1 and E, twice the amount of vitamin B2, minerals, and oil. Brown rice needs a brief rinse under cold, running water to remove anything that floats to the surface. Leave the rinsed rice in a bowl of clean water for at least 2–3 hours, but ideally overnight. The amount of water needed to cook the rice depends on how long the rice has been soaked; the shorter the soaking time, the more water is required for cooking. If the rice has been left to soak overnight, add 20 percent more water than the weight of rice. In other words, if you have 3 1/2 ounces/2/3 cup of rice, add 1/2 cup water. Use as solid and heavy a saucepan as possible, with a sturdy lid. Put the rice and water in the pan with the lid on and bring to a boil over very low heat. Turn up the heat to medium when steam starts to escape and cook until the steam begins to slow down. Turn off the heat, but do not remove the lid. Leave to steam in the retained heat for 10–15 minutes longer before fluffing the rice.

Asparagus & anchovy domburi

Serves 2

- 1 tablespoon vegetable oil
- 2 anchovy fillets, chopped
- 1 teaspoon finely minced garlic
- 6 asparagus spears, cut diagonally into bite-size pieces
- 2 tablespoons water
- 2 tablespoons onion soy-dashi sauce (page 40)
- 1/4 teaspoon agar agar, dissolved in 1 teaspoon water
- 2/3 cup warm, cooked rice (see above)
- 1 teaspoon toasted sesame seeds, roughly ground

Asparagus is a highly seasonal vegetable, so I try to eat as much of it as possible when it is available. In this quick-and-easy recipe, all the asparagus flavor is captured in the sauce.

Heat the oil in a frying pan over medium heat and sauté the anchovies first, then add the garlic and asparagus. Lower the heat slightly and add the water and the onion soy-dashi sauce to season. When the cooking liquid starts to boil, add the agar agar to thicken the sauce.

Put the rice in warmed bowls, top with the asparagus mixture, and sprinkle over the sesame seeds. Serve with chopsticks.

Zucchini & tomato domburi

Serves 2

- 1 tablespoon olive oil
- 2 medium zucchini, peeled and diced
- 2 anchovy fillets, roughly chopped
- 1 garlic clove, finely minced
- 4 tablespoons tomato juice
- 2 tablespoons sake
- 2 teaspoons soy sauce
- 1 tablespoon miso paste
- 1¼ cups warm, cooked rice (page 31)
- a few sprigs of flat-leaf parsley, finely chopped

This is a fast summer dish with a Japanese twist. Be sure to get very fresh and plump zucchini.

Put the oil in a pan over a medium heat and sauté the zucchini for 1 minute. Add the anchovies and garlic, shaking the pan a few times.

Reduce the heat slightly and add the tomato sauce, sake, and soy sauce to season. Let the cooking liquid come to a boil, turn off the heat, and stir in the miso paste.

Divide the rice between two warmed bowls, top with the zucchini mixture, garnish with the chopped parsley, and serve with chopsticks.

Egg & spinach domburi

Serves 2

- ½ leek, trimmed
- ⅔ cup water
- 1 cup baby spinach leaves
- 2 tablespoons sake
- 2 tablespoons mirin
- ½ tablespoon sugar
- 3 tablespoons soy sauce
- 2 eggs, lightly beaten
- 1¼ cups warm, cooked rice (page 31)
- a small handful of shredded nori (optional)

Egg is a classic ingredient for domburi topping since it is quick and versatile. To achieve the correct consistency for domburi toppings, the eggs should be cooked until just before they set, so that the egg binds the other ingredients together while still retaining enough moisture to act as a sauce over the rice.

Cut the leek lengthwise and finely slice diagonally. Place the leek and the water in a saucepan and bring to a boil over medium-low heat.

Lower the heat slightly and add the spinach, sake, mirin, sugar, and soy sauce. Gently pour in the beaten eggs and stir. Turn off the heat when the egg mixture just starts to set and serve over the rice. Garnish with the shredded nori and serve immediately.

Tip
Try not to overcook. It is better to stop cooking earlier rather than later as the retained heat will continue to cook the eggs.

Chile mushrooms & tofu domburi

Serves 2

- ½ (12-ounce) package firm tofu
- 6 medium cremini mushrooms
- 4 shiitake mushrooms
- 4 ounces fresh shimeji mushrooms
  (or more cremini and shiitakes)
- ½ tablespoon vegetable oil
- ½ onion, finely minced
- 2 teaspoons grated or finely
  minced ginger
- 1 garlic clove, finely minced
- ¼–½ large red chile, deseeded and
  finely chopped
- 2 tablespoons sake
- 1 tablespoon soy sauce
- 1 tablespoon medium-colored or
  red miso paste
- 1 teaspoon chile sauce (optional)
- 1¼ cups warm, cooked rice
  (page 31)

This is a gutsy, wholesome vegetarian dish that is sure to leave you feeling very satisfied. Adjust the amount of chiles to suit your heat tolerance.

Start by dicing the tofu into ½-inch cubes. Blanch them in boiling water and drain.

Cut the cremini mushrooms into quarters. Cut the shiitake mushrooms into wedges the same size as the cremini mushroom quarters, discarding the stems. Cut off the jointed base of the shimeji mushrooms and separate.

Heat the oil in a pan over low heat and sweat the onion until soft. Add the tofu, ginger, garlic, chile, and mushrooms and cook for 2–3 minutes. Add the sake and soy sauce to season and let the cooking liquid start to bubble.

Turn off the heat and stir in the miso paste. Taste and adjust the seasoning. If you like more heat, add the chile sauce. Divide the rice between two bowls, spoon the mushroom mixture over the rice, and serve with chopsticks.

Seafood & wild arugula domburi

This is a fusion-flavored domburi dish—part Italian and part Thai, and very quick and easy to make.

Make shallow incisions over the body of the squid and cut into bite-size pieces. Chop the tentacles into pieces of a manageable length. Put both the squid and the shrimp in a bowl, and sprinkle with the cornstarch and salt.

Heat the olive oil in a pan over low heat and add the garlic. Add the shrimp and squid and sauté until opaque. Season with the chile flakes and nam pla. Turn off the heat and quickly stir in the arugula leaves to wilt in the residual heat.

Put the rice into two warmed bowls, and top with the seafood mixture. Serve with chopsticks.

Serves 2

- 3$\frac{1}{2}$ ounces small cleaned squid
- 3$\frac{1}{2}$ ounces peeled, uncooked shrimp
- 2 teaspoons cornstarch
- $\frac{1}{2}$ teaspoon salt
- 2 tablespoons olive oil
- 1 garlic clove, finely minced
- pinch of chile flakes
- 2 teaspoons nam pla (Thai fish sauce)
- $\frac{1}{2}$ cup arugula leaves, roughly chopped
- 1$\frac{1}{4}$ cups warm, cooked rice (page 31)

Fava bean & crabmeat domburi

The sweetness of the fava beans and the crabmeat are perfectly matched in this recipe.

Cook the fava beans for 2–3 minutes in boiling water. Drain, rinse in cold water, and then remove their outer skin (I am sorry, this is rather fiddly, but the result is well worth the extra effort!).

Place the fava beans and crabmeat in a saucepan with the sake and bring to a boil over medium heat. Season with salt and white pepper to taste. Add the dissolved agar agar to thicken the cooking liquid.

Put the rice into two warmed bowls, top with the fava bean mixture, and garnish with the grated zest. Serve with chopsticks.

Serves 2

- $\frac{2}{3}$ cup fresh fava beans (shelled weight)
- $\frac{1}{2}$ cup lump crabmeat
- 4 tablespoons sake
- $\frac{1}{4}$ teaspoon agar agar, dissolved in 1 teaspoon water
- 1$\frac{1}{4}$ cups warm, cooked rice (page 31)
- 1 teaspoon finely grated lemon or lime zest
- salt and freshly ground white pepper

Spiced lentils with shrimp

This is a wonderful combination of flavors and because it's so easy to make, it's a great lunch dish for busy people who need to eat well.

Serves 2

- 1 cup Puy lentils
- ²/₃ cup frozen sweet corn
- 2 scallions, finely chopped
- 2 vine-ripened tomatoes, deseeded and roughly chopped
- ½ green chile, deseeded and finely chopped
- a handful of fresh cilantro, finely chopped
- 2 tablespoons soy sauce
- 2 tablespoons extra-virgin olive oil
- 7 ounces cooked, peeled shrimp
- salt and freshly ground black pepper

Put the lentils in a saucepan, cover with water, and cook over medium heat for 20–25 minutes, or until the lentils are soft but not mushy. Drain, rinse under cold, running water, and drain well. Cook the corn for 3–5 minutes and drain.

In a bowl, mix together the lentils, corn, scallions, tomatoes, chile, and cilantro. Add the soy sauce and olive oil and adjust the seasoning to taste with salt and pepper.

Divide the lentil mixture between two serving plates, arrange the shrimp on top, and serve with chopsticks.

Tuna, tomato, & okra domburi

I have used canned tuna here for ease, but of course if you have a delicious tuna steak in the fridge, treat yourself for lunch.

Serves 2

- 6 okra pods
- 2 vine-ripened tomatoes, peeled and roughly chopped
- ¼ cup flaked canned tuna
- 2 tablespoons onion soy-dashi sauce (page 40)
- salt and and freshly ground black pepper
- 1¼ cups warm cooked rice (page 31)
- a few basil leaves, finely torn

Sprinkle a pinch of salt on the okra and rub them gently together to remove the very fine hairs. Blanch the okra quickly, discarding the tops, then slice into ⅙ inch pieces. Place the okra slices in a bowl. Season with salt and pepper. Stir to develop the characteristic stickiness.

Add the tomatoes, tuna, and the onion soy-dashi sauce. Stir to combine the mixture and season.

Put the rice into two bowls, top with the tomato and okra mixture, and garnish with basil. Serve with chopsticks.

Warm lentils with tofu & spinach

Serves 2

For the onion soy-dashi sauce
- 1 cup soy sauce
- 1 cup mirin
- 1/2 onion, grated
- 1 garlic clove, grated
- 2-inch square piece of konbu

- 1 cup Puy lentils
- 2 garlic cloves, slightly crushed with the side of a knife
- 1 red bell pepper
- 1 yellow bell pepper
- 1/4 (12-ounce) package firm tofu
- 2 cups baby spinach leaves, washed and drained
- 2 tablespoons onion soy-dashi sauce (see above)
- 1 tablespoon good-quality balsamic vinegar
- 1 tablespoon extra-virgin olive oil

The slightly peppery-tasting Puy lentils and gentle tofu are a perfect match in this sustaining lunch dish.

To make the onion soy-dashi sauce, place all the ingredients for the sauce in a saucepan and bring to a boil over low heat. Reduce the heat and simmer for 8–10 minutes. Turn off the heat and let the sauce cool down before straining it through a fine-mesh sieve. The sauce will keep for 2 weeks refrigerated in a glass bottle. This is a tasty, versatile sauce that features in other recipes.

Put the lentils in a saucepan, cover with water, add the garlic, and bring to a boil. Reduce the heat and simmer for 20–25 minutes, or until the lentils are soft but not mushy. Remove the garlic, drain, and set the lentils aside, covered to keep warm.

Place the peppers under a preheated broiler, turning occasionally until the skins blacken. When the skins are completely black, put the peppers inside a resealable plastic bag to sweat, then remove the peel and discard the seeds. Reserve the juices and slice the flesh into thin strips.

While the peppers are broiling, wrap the tofu in paper towel and microwave on medium for 1 minute to drain. Dice the tofu into bite-size cubes.

Put the spinach, lentils, peppers with the juices, and tofu in a mixing bowl. Pour over the onion soy-dashi sauce, balsamic vinegar, and olive oil. Gently stir to mix and serve with chopsticks.

Stir-fry soybeans with spicy miso

Serves 2

- $1/2$ cup dried soybeans, soaked overnight (see Tip)
- $1/2$ tablespoon vegetable oil
- 2 ounces ground pork
- 1 onion, finely minced
- 1 carrot, finely chopped
- 1 garlic clove, crushed and finely minced
- 1 tablespoon sake
- 1 tablespoon soy sauce
- 1 tablespoon chile sauce
- 2 tablespoons medium-colored miso paste
- $1 1/4$ cups warm, cooked rice (page 31)
- 1 scallion, finely chopped diagonally
- a small handful of watercress

You need to soak the beans overnight then simmer for about an hour. I am afraid it is a rather lengthy process, so I recommend cooking a large quantity and freezing what you don't use. Or, if you are in hurry, use canned soybeans, which are now widely available.

Drain the soybeans, place in a pan covered with fresh water, and cook over medium heat for 45–60 minutes. Reserve $1/4$ cup of the cooking water.

Heat a wok over medium heat, add the oil and stir-fry the pork for 3 minutes. Add the onion and carrot and cook for 2 minutes before adding the garlic to cook for 3 minutes longer.

Reduce the heat slightly and add the soybeans, reserved cooking water, sake, and soy sauce. Continue to cook while stirring constantly until the cooking liquid has almost evaporated. Turn off the heat, then stir in the chile sauce and miso paste. Mix well to incorporate.

Divide the rice between two bowls, top with the bean mixture, and garnish with the scallion and watercress. Serve with chopsticks.

Tip

If you are using canned soybeans, use $1/2$ (15-ounce) can and add $1/4$ cup water.

Soba noodles with napa cabbage & tofu

Serves 2

- 1 postcard-size piece of konbu
- 7 ounces dried soba noodles
- 2 tablespoons olive oil
- 1½ cups finely chopped napa cabbage
- ½ teaspoon salt
- 1 tablespoon toasted white sesame seeds, finely ground
- ¼ (12-ounce) package soft silken tofu, diced
- 1 tablespoon soymilk
- 1 tablespoon white miso paste
- 1 teaspoon toasted white sesame seeds

Try to use soba noodles when making these recipes as they are the most healthy of noodles. This is a gentle, beautifully creamy noodle sauce made with tofu, sesame seeds, and white miso. In spite of appearing mild, it is packed with flavor and high-quality vegetable proteins.

Put the konbu in a saucepan of cold water and bring to a simmer over low heat. Take the konbu out when it floats to the surface and the water begins to boil. Take out a ladleful of water and reserve it for later. Let the water come back to a rolling boil.

Add the noodles and stir to separate them. Pour in a glass of cold water when the water begins to rise to the top of the saucepan. The noodles are ready when the water returns to a boil. Drain, rinse under cold, running water, and set aside to drain well.

Put the olive oil in a frying pan and cook the napa cabbage over medium heat. Sprinkle in the salt to encourage the napa cabbage to soften. When it is soft, add the reserved konbu water, ground sesame seeds, tofu, and soymilk. Simmer and reduce for 5–8 minutes.

Add the miso paste and stir well to mix. Put the soba noodles in the sauce and stir to combine.

Turn off the heat, divide the noodles between two serving plates, sprinkle with the sesame seeds, and serve with chopsticks.

Wakame & spinach soba noodles with sesame dipping sauce

Serves 2

- 1½ ounces dried wakame
- 7 ounces dried soba noodles
- 7 ounces spinach, cut into stems and leaves, washed and drained
- 1 scallion, finely chopped diagonally
- 2 tablespoons shredded nori
- Japanese seven-spice chili powder or chile flakes (optional)

For the sesame dipping sauce
- 4 tablespoons toasted sesame seeds
- 4 tablespoons onion soy-dashi sauce (page 40)
- ½ cup water

Spinach is a super health food—it is packed with vitamins B and C, anticancerous beta-carotene, and various minerals, especially iron. In this recipe you get the double benefits of both wakame and spinach.

Put the wakame in a bowl of water at room temperature to soften for 5 minutes and then drain.

To prepare the dipping sauce, put the sesame seeds in a mortar and grind them to a coarse powder. Add the onion soy-dashi sauce and dilute with the water. Divide the sauce mixture into two cups and set aside.

Bring a large saucepan of water to a boil over high heat and add the soba noodles. Stir to separate the noodles. Adjust the heat if necessary to prevent the water from boiling over and cook the noodles for 2–3 minutes. Then add the spinach, stems first, adding the soft leaves, along with the wakame, afterward.

Just as the water comes back to a boil and begins to rise, turn off the heat and quickly drain in a sieve. Run the sieve under cold, running water to refresh the noodles and the vegetables.

Drain well and divide between two serving plates. Garnish with the chopped scallion, shredded nori, and chili powder, if using. Serve with the dipping sauce and chopsticks.

Soba noodles with pickled plums & sprouting broccoli

Serves 2

- 7 ounces dried soba noodles
- 2 tablespoons extra-virgin olive oil
- 2 garlic cloves, thinly sliced
- 1/4 teaspoon salt
- 2 1/2 cups sprouting broccoli, cut into bite-size pieces
- 2 umeboshi (pickled plums), pitted and chopped
- 1/2 tablespoon toasted sesame seeds

Pickled plums are called umeboshi in Japanese, and are a staple in Japanese kitchen cupboards because they are believed to be an edible cure-all.

Bring a large saucepan of water to a boil, add the noodles, and stir to separate them. At the same time, heat the oil, garlic, and salt in a generous-sized frying pan over low heat to infuse the oil with garlic flavor.

When the saucepan of water comes back to a boil, add the broccoli to cook for 1 minute. Pour in a glass of cold water when the water starts to rise to the top. Let the water return to a boil for the third time, then turn off the heat. Drain and rinse under cold, running water. Drain well again. Take the garlic out of the frying pan and add the noodle mixture to briefly sauté.

Turn off the heat, add the umeboshi, and stir together. Divide the noodle mixture onto two dishes, sprinkle with the sesame seeds to garnish, and serve with chopsticks.

Baked eggplant with grated daikon on green tea soba noodles

Serves 2

- 1 eggplant, pricked
- 7 ounces dried green tea soba noodles
- ½ large daikon radish, scrubbed clean
- 4 tablespoons onion soy-dashi sauce (page 40)
- 2 teaspoons grated ginger

This is another recipe with the wonderfully refreshing grated daikon, which counterbalances the rich taste of eggplant. Try and use green tea–infused soba noodles, so you gain all the nutrtional benefits of green tea as well as the goodness of the soba noodles.

Place the eggplant under a broiler preheated to its highest setting and turn it until blackened all over. When the eggplant is cool enough to handle, peel it by running a bamboo skewer just beneath the skin. Cut the flesh into strips and set aside.

Bring a saucepan of water to a boil, add the noodles, and stir to separate the strands. When the water comes back to a boil and begins to rise to the top, pour in a glass of cold water. Let the water return to a boil for a third time, then drain, rinse under cold, running water, and drain again.

Meanwhile, grate the daikon and squeeze gently in your hand, fluff up the pulp, and reserve the juice. Mix the juice with the onion soy-dashi sauce and stir in the grated ginger.

Divide the noodles into two equal portions on serving dishes and pour the onion soy-dashi sauce over. Put the grated daikon over the noodles and top with the eggplant strips. Serve with chopsticks.

Nori & arugula soba in broth

This is an updated version of a classic soba noodle dish called hanamaki soba, which is a simple soba in broth with just-crushed nori. This noodle sauce can accompany many noodle dishes—use it as a base to create your own healthy variations.

Serves 2

For the noodle sauce
- 1 postcard-size piece of konbu
- 7 tablespoons soy sauce
- 4 tablespoons sugar
- 2 tablespoons mirin

- 7 ounces dried soba noodles
- 2 cups arugula leaves
- 1 postcard-size piece of konbu
- 2 sheets nori
- 2 scallions, finely chopped
- ½ teaspoon chile flakes

To prepare the noodle sauce, place the konbu in a saucepan with all the other ingredients and set aside for at least 30 minutes, but ideally 1 hour, before heating it over low heat.

Take the konbu out and simmer for 5–7 minutes before turning off the heat. Let it cool to room temperature and refrigerate in a sterilized glass jar with a lid. The sauce will keep for 4 weeks in the fridge. The sauce is used as a base for noodle broth, or as a noodle-dipping sauce.

Bring a saucepan of water to a boil, add the noodles, and stir to separate the strands. When the water comes back to a boil and begins to rise to the top, pour in a glass of cold water. Let the water return to a boil for a third time, drain, rinse under cold, running water, and drain again. Divide the noodles into two bowls with the arugula leaves.

Meanwhile, put the konbu in a saucepan with 1¼ cups water and bring to a simmer over low heat. Take the konbu out just before the water reaches a boil, add 4 tablespoons of the noodle sauce, and let it come to a boil. Turn off the heat and ladle the broth over the noodles.

Crush the nori with your hands over the bowls of noodles, garnish with the scallions, sprinkle with the chile flakes, and serve immediately with chopsticks.

Japanese mushrooms with soba noodles in green tea broth

Mushrooms are generally low in calories, contain no fat, are rich in edible fiber and packed with flavor. These mysterious fungi are a tasty ally for dieters. In this recipe, I combine the smoky flavor of Japanese mushrooms with refreshing green tea to make a wonderful, healthy noodle broth.

Start by preparing the green tea mix by finely grinding the sesame seeds with a pestle and mortar. Add the remaining ingredients and grind the mixture further to incorporate completely.

Slice the shiitake mushrooms, discarding the stems. Cut off the bases of both the shimeji and enoki mushrooms where they join, and separate them. Pull the oyster mushrooms into strips with your hands.

Mix the water with the noodle sauce in a saucepan, add the mushrooms, and cook over medium heat. Lower the heat so the broth doesn't boil. Add the green tea mix and the agar agar to thicken.

Meanwhile, bring a saucepan of water to a boil, add the noodles, and stir to separate the strands. When the water comes back to a boil and begins to rise to the top, pour in a glass of cold water. Let the water return to a boil for a third time, drain, rinse under cold, running water, and drain again.

Divide the noodles into two warm bowls, pour over the broth, garnish with the scallions, and serve immediately with chopsticks.

Serves 2

For the green tea mix
- 2 tablespoons toasted black sesame seeds, finely ground
- 1 tablespoon matcha (green tea powder)
- 2 tablespoons kinako (soybean flour)
- 2 tablespoons dark brown sugar

- 4 fresh shiitake mushrooms
- 3 1/2 ounces shimeji mushrooms
- 3 1/2 ounces enoki mushrooms
- 6 medium oyster mushrooms
- 1 1/4 cups water
- 4 tablespoons noodle sauce (page 50)
- 2 teaspoons green tea mix (see above)
- 1/4 teaspoon agar agar powder, dissolved in 1 teaspoon water
- 7 ounces dried soba noodles
- 2 scallions, finely chopped

Tip
The green tea mix will keep for up to 4 weeks in an airtight container placed in the fridge. It makes a wonderful hot drink substitute for coffee.

Chilled soba noodles with gazpacho sauce

Serves 2

- 7 ounces dried soba noodles
- 1 tablespoon extra-virgin olive oil

For the gazpacho sauce
- $1/2$ cup tomato juice
- $1/2$ white or red onion, finely chopped
- $1/2$ red bell pepper, finely chopped
- $1/2$ yellow bell pepper, finely chopped
- 1 celery stalk, finely chopped
- $1/2$ baby cucumber, chopped
- salt and freshly ground black pepper
- a few sprigs of flat-leaf parsley, finely chopped

This is a vibrant, fresh tomato-based pasta sauce that goes perfectly with Japanese soba noodles. Trust me, you will love it.

Bring a saucepan of water to a boil, add the noodles, and stir to separate the strands. When the water comes back to a boil and begins to rise to the top, pour in a glass of cold water. Let the water return to a boil for a third time, drain, rinse under cold, running water, coat the noodles with the oil to stop them from sticking together, and refrigerate in a colander over a bowl to drain further while you make the sauce.

Put all the ingredients for the sauce in a big bowl and stir to combine. Take out a couple of tablespoons of the sauce and set aside. Add the noodles to the bowl and mix.

Arrange the noodle mixture on two serving plates, top with the reserved sauce, garnish with the chopped parsley, and serve with chopsticks.

Seared scallops & soba noodles with mizuna pesto

Serves 2

For the mizuna pesto
- 2 cups mizuna leaves, roughly chopped
- 2 tablespoons pine nuts
- 1 garlic clove, crushed
- 1/2 teaspoon wasabi paste
- 1/2 teaspoon salt
- 4 tablespoons extra-virgin olive oil, plus extra for drizzling

- 4 large fresh diver scallops
- 2 teaspoons vegetable oil
- 7 ounces dried soba noodles
- 1 cup arugula leaves
- 1 1/2 tablespoons mizuna pesto (see above)
- 1 scallion, finely chopped

Mizuna is a highly decorative, green, leafy vegetable that originates in both China and Japan. It grows in a bushy clump of big green rosettes; the upper part resembles serrated wild arugula leaves, while the lower part of each leaf is a slender and firm white stalk. Mizuna also tastes similar to peppery wild arugula but has a juicier, crunchy texture.

Nutritionally, mizuna is about 95 percent water and contains high levels of vitamins A and C, which are both good for the skin. It also contains various minerals, including calcium and iron.

It is getting easier to find in Asian grocers, especially in the winter and autumn, but a mixture of arugula and spinach makes a good substitute in this recipe.

Make the mizuna pesto by putting all the ingredients for the pesto in a food processor and blending until smooth. It will make about 2/3 cup. Transfer to a plastic container, drizzle over some olive oil to cover the top surface, replace the lid, and refrigerate to keep for up to 1 week.

Preheat a cast-iron grill pan over medium heat. Split the scallops in half horizontally, brush with oil, and grill for 20–30 seconds on each side. Transfer to a plate to keep warm.

Meanwhile, bring a saucepan of water to a boil, add the noodles, and stir to separate the strands. When the water returns to a boil and begins to rise to the top, add a glass of cold water and let it return to a boil for the third time. Drain and rinse under hot, running water and drain well again. Put the noodles back into the same saucepan (which should be still warm), add the arugula leaves and the pesto, and stir to mix evenly.

Divide the noodles between two serving plates, arrange the scallops on the top and garnish with the scallion. Serve with chopsticks.

Swirling egg soba noodles in broth

This pretty noodle dish is quick to make and so it's useful as a recipe to have up your sleeve when you want an instant lunch.

Mix the water with the noodle sauce in a saucepan. Bring to just below a boil over medium heat, add the agar agar to thicken the broth, and lower the heat to a simmer.

Serves 2

- 1¼ cups water
- 4 tablespoons noodle sauce (page 50)
- ½ teaspoon agar agar powder, dissolved in 2 teaspoons water
- 7 ounces dried soba noodles
- 1 egg, lightly beaten
- 1 sheet nori, crushed into small pieces
- 2 sprigs of watercress
- 2 teaspoons grated ginger

Bring another saucepan of water to a boil, add the noodles, and stir to separate the strands. When the water comes back to a boil and begins to rise to the top, pour in a glass of cold water. Let the water return to a boil for a third time, drain, rinse under cold, running water, and drain again.

Pour the beaten egg into the broth. Wait for a moment and then stir with a pair of chopsticks, swirling the egg. Turn off the heat.

Divide the noodles between two warm bowls and ladle the broth over them. Garnish with the crushed nori, watercress, and small mounds of grated ginger. Serve immediately with chopsticks.

Sobaghetti with broccoli & tofu

A really simple lunch for when you haven't got much in the fridge—so much better than grabbing a sandwich from the local shop, with all those hidden fats and nasties!

Serves 2

- 4 ounces firm cotton tofu
- 2 garlic cloves, sliced
- 1 teaspoon salt
- 7 ounces dried soba noodles
- 1 tablespoon olive oil
- 1 head of broccoli, weighing around 7 ounces, roughly chopped
- salt and freshly ground black pepper
- 1 tablespoon toasted sesame seeds
- a big handful of shredded nori

Drain the tofu by wrapping it in paper towel and microwaving for 1 minute on medium, and roughly chop.

Put the garlic and salt in a saucepan with plenty of water to bring to a boil over a medium heat. Cook the garlic for 2–3 minutes before adding the broccoli to cook for 3 minutes longer. Drain (but reserve a ladle of cooking water) and rinse under cold running water and drain well.

Meanwhile, bring another saucepan of water to a boil, add the noodles and stir to separate the strands. When the water comes back to a boil and begins to rise to the top, pour in a glass of cold water. Let the water return to a boil for a third time, drain, rinse under cold running water, and drain again.

Put the olive oil in a pan over medium heat. Add the garlic, broccoli, and tofu and, with a back of fork, squash the garlic and broccoli and add the reserved cooking water. When the broccoli mixture begins to bubble, add the soba noodles and stir to incorporate the noodles with the broccoli mixture. Season with the salt and pepper and divide between two serving plates. Garnish with the sesame seeds and shredded nori and serve immediately with chopsticks.

Salmon roe & grated daikon soba noodles

Daikon has become easier to find in supermarkets. It is a low-calorie vegetable rich in vitamins, particularly A and C, and is known as a natural digestive. It also has a refreshing astringent taste. The easiest and the most effective way to get the full benefits is to eat it raw. Choose one that feels firm and solid, with no bruises.

Serves 2

- 1 white or red onion, thinly sliced
- ½ large daikon radish, scrubbed clean
- 4 tablespoons onion soy-dashi sauce (page 40)
- 4 tablespoons salmon roe
- 1 tablespoon sake
- 7 ounces dried soba noodles (preferably green tea–infused soba)
- 2 teaspoons wasabi powder, mixed with 4 teaspoons water

Start by soaking the onion slices in a bowl of cold water to reduce their aroma and refresh them. Grate the daikon, skin and all. Squeeze gently in your hand, fluff up the pulp, and reserve the juice. Mix the juice with the onion soy-dashi sauce. Mix the salmon roe with the sake.

Bring a saucepan of water to a boil, add the noodles, and stir to separate the strands. When the water comes back to a boil and begins to rise to the top, pour in a glass of cold water. Let the water return to a boil for a third time, drain, rinse under cold, running water, and drain again.

Drain the onion slices. Divide the soba noodles between two serving plates and pour the diluted onion soy-dashi sauce over them. Arrange the onion, grated daikon, and salmon roe on top of each bowl. Serve with a small mound of wasabi paste in the middle, and chopsticks.

Today life seems so hectic we barely have time to sit down for lunch. We are often forced into grabbing a pre-packed sandwich from the corner deli or grocery store. While better than no lunch at all, a store-bought lunch can be pretty doubtful—it's likely high in calories and fat, and, above all, you have no control over the quality of the ingredients.

It takes only a little forward planning to make yourself a delicious and healthy packed lunch that will sustain you until the evening, as you'll discover with these recipes. Many recipes from the preceding chapter of One-bowl Lunch are also interchangeable to turn into movable meals.

Lunch on-the-go

Rolled sushi

Serves 1

- a sheet of nori
- $^2/_3$ cup prepared sushi rice (page 132)
- a small bowl of water
- wasabi paste

For the filling, choose from the following and cut into pencil-size strips

- fresh or cooked vegetables such as cucumber, carrot, asparagus, or green beans
- sashimi-grade fresh fish such as tuna, salmon, sea bass, or plaice
- smoked salmon

Equipment

- rolling mat

Rolled sushi is an ideal food-to-go. The rolling technique may seem a little tricky initially to those who are unaccustomed to it, but with a little perseverance and practice, rolling sushi will soon become as easy as making sandwiches. The key to successful rolling is to make sure you have all the ingredients and equipment at hand and are organized.

Halve a sheet of nori and place it on a rolling mat, smooth and shiny side face down, in front of you. Wet your hands in the bowl of water, take the prepared sushi rice, and form it into a sausage shape.

Place the rice on the nori and spread it evenly over the sheet, leaving a 1/4 inch margin along the top edge. The margin is for the overlap.

With your right index finger, smear a line of the wasabi paste across the center of the rice and place a piece of filling (which you have cut into pencil-size strips) on top.

With both of your thumbs and index fingers, lift up the near side edge of the rolling mat while keeping the filling in place with your middle and third fingers. Bring the near side edge of the rice to meet the top edge of the rice and roll.

Open the rolling mat to reveal a roll, cover the roll with the mat again, and gently run your hands along from the center to the outer edges to shape the roll into a neat cylinder.

To cut a rolled sushi, place it on a chopping board, wet the blade of a sharp kitchen knife, and cut it in half. Put the two halved rolls next to each other, in parallel, and cut them into three equal-length pieces. You should now have six perfectly sized rolled sushi pieces.

Stuffed sushi

Serves 1

For the seasoned, deep-fried tofu pouches
- 2 deep-fried tofu pouches
- boiling water, to cover
- 7 tablespoons water
- 1 tablespoon sugar
- 2 tablespoons soy sauce
- 1 tablespoon mirin

For the deep-fried, tofu-stuffed sushi
- 4 seasoned, deep-fried tofu pouches (see above)
- 1 tablespoon sushi pickled ginger, finely chopped
- 2 teaspoons toasted sesame seeds
- 1½ cups prepared sushi rice (page 132)

Sweet, seasoned, deep-fried tofu is the classic choice for stuffed sushi. Although ready-made seasoned, deep-fried tofu pouches are available and they are a handy pantry standby, I always prefer the homemade ones. The seasoned tofu will keep for 4–5 days, if refrigerated, or for up to a month, if frozen.

Cut the deep-fried tofu pouches in half and pour boiling water over them to get rid of any excess oil. Carefully separate each half deep-fried tofu to make a pouch. Put all the tofu pouches in a saucepan with the water and sugar. Bring to a boil and cook for 3 minutes over medium-high heat.

Add the soy sauce and mirin and reduce the heat to low to simmer until most of the liquid has evaporated.

To make the deep-fried, tofu-stuffed sushi, gently pat dry the tofu pouches to get rid of any excess liquid. Mix the sushi ginger and the sesame seeds with the sushi rice and divide into four equal portions. With a moist tablespoon, put the rice in each tofu pouch and fold over the top edge to enclose.

Salmon furikake (sprinkles)

Furikake (sprinkles) are very easy to prepare and make a healthy accompaniment to rice in a bento box (Japanese lunch box). Cook the ingredients in a dry frying pan to remove any moisture.

Serves 1

- ½ teaspoon salt
- 3 ounces salmon fillet
- 1 teaspoon light soy sauce
- 1½ tablespoons toasted sesame seeds
- ½ sheet of nori, finely shredded
- ⅔ cup cooled, cooked rice (page 31)

Rub the salt over the salmon, refrigerate for 30 minutes, then broil until cooked to your liking. Remove and discard the skin, then break the flesh into fine flakes with your hands. Put the salmon flakes in a nonstick frying pan with the soy sauce and cook while stirring with two pairs of chopsticks over low heat until all the moisture has evaporated. Add the sesame seeds and nori. Mix well to incorporate, then let the sprinkles cool down.

Put the cooled rice in a bento box and cover with the cooled sprinkles.

Wakame and green tea furikake (sprinkles)

Serves 1

- ½ ounce dried wakame
- 1 tablespoon green tea leaves (preferably high-grade gyokuro variety)
- 1 tablespoon toasted sesame seeds
- ⅔ cup cooled, cooked rice (page 31)

To store the sprinkles, transfer to a container to refrigerate. The sprinkles will keep for 7 days in the fridge.

With a pestle and mortar, finely grind both the dried wakame and the tea together.

Heat a nonstick frying pan over low heat, then add the wakame and tea and cook until the mixture becomes crisp. Add the sesame seeds and let the sprinkles cool down.

Put the cooled rice in a bento box and cover with the cooled sprinkles.

Omusubi (rice balls)

Makes 1

- 2 teaspoons salt
- 7 tablespoons cold water
- 2/3 cup warm, cooked sushi rice (page 31)
- a sheet of nori

For the filling, choose one of the following:
- umeboshi (pickled plums), pitted
- takuan (yellow pickled radish), chopped
- ready-made pickles of your choice, drained
- small pieces of grilled fish
- chopped smoked salmon

Omusubi is a popular and classic takeout food in Japan. Warm rice is neatly shaped into various shapes with a small amount of filling in the center, wrapped or covered with different dry ingredients. The choices of fillings and wrapping materials are almost endless. Once you have mastered the technique, I'm sure you will enjoy both making and eating omusubi. Here is how to make triangular omusubi, wrapped in nori. Usually the rice surrounds the filling, but as in the photograph you can make them so you can see the filling on one side.

In a bowl, dissolve the salt in the water. Moisten both hands with the salt water.

Reserving 2 teaspoons of the rice, put the remaining rice on your left palm and gently squeeze. Make an indentation in the center, put in a filling of your choice (an umeboshi is the classic choice), and cover the filling with the reserved rice. With your right index and middle finger cupped over the rice in your left hand, shape the rice into a neat triangle.

Place the rice triangle on one of the nori triangles. Bring up the bottom edge of the nori to cover the omusubi. Fold both left and right edges of the nori over the sides of the omusubi, leaving only the top tip of the omusubi uncovered. Repeat with the remaining rice and nori triangle.

Fresh spring rolls

- 4 sheets of rice paper, soaked in water to soften
- 1 small cucumber
- 1 small carrot
- ½ avocado
- 2 tablespoons yofu (tofu yogurt)
- 1 teaspoon medium-colored miso paste
- ½ teaspoon wasabi paste
- 4 lettuce leaves, trimmed
- 4 ounces cooked peeled shrimp

Rice paper is made from rice flour; it is low in calories and has no fat. It is also very quick and easy to use, which makes rice paper ideal for making a quick lunch to go.

Pat the rice paper sheets dry and keep them separated in layers of moistened paper towels while you prepare the vegetables.

Cut the cucumber into quarters lengthwise and discard the seeds. Peel the carrot and cut into 4 pencil-size sticks. Cut the avocado into 4 strips. Mix the yofu with the miso and wasabi pastes.

Put the rice papers on a clean chopping board. Divide the lettuce, cucumber, carrot, avocado, and shrimp among them. Spoon the yofu mix over the vegetables and roll. Cut each spring roll in half diagonally and pack in lunch boxes.

You may be surprised to know that salads are not part of the traditional Japanese cooking repertoire. Instead Japanese cuisine has sunomono (literally "vinegared things") and aemono ("combined" or "harmonized" things). Small portions of sunomono and aemono are normally served as side dishes in elegant bowls or stylish dishes. There is great scope for creativity in incorporating the traditional Japanese techniques of sunomono and aemono using ingredients such as rice vinegar, soy sauce, and miso. All of the following recipes are designed as one-course meals either for lunch or supper. Some recipes are more filling than others and you need to adjust the balance between lunch and evening meal. Many recipes using daikon can easily be made more substantial by increasing the amount of daikon as it is 95 percent water and has a very low calorie count. And of course, if you do find yourself feeling peckish there is always delicious guilt-free snacks to help you through in the Hunger Busters chapter later.

Salads

Potato, green bean, tomato, & spinach salad with minty soy dressing

Serves 2

- 6 baby new potatoes, scrubbed clean
- 100g fine green beans, trimmed and halved
- 1/2 red onion, thinly sliced
- 1 garlic clove, halved
- 10 baby vine-ripened tomatoes, halved
- 2 cups small spinach leaves
- 1 teaspoon toasted sesame seeds

For the minty soy dressing
- 4 tablespoons soy sauce
- 1 tablespoon runny honey
- 1 tablespoon rice vinegar
- 1 teaspoon sesame oil
- a handful of fresh mint leaves, finely shredded

This is the kind of salad lunch I enjoy eating on a warm day. It is beautiful to look at and full of summer garden tastes.

Cut the potatoes into thick slices and boil for 10 minutes. Blanch the beans for 2–3 minutes, refresh under cold, running water, and set aside to drain well. Soak the onion slices (to rid them of their smell) in a bowl of cold water for 10 minutes and drain.

Rub the garlic on the surface of two serving bowls or plates. Mix together all the ingredients for the dressing.

Put all the vegetables in a bowl, pour in the dressing, toss, and divide between the serving bowls. Sprinkle with the sesame seeds, and serve with chopsticks.

Asparagus, green bean, & hijiki soba noodle salad

Serves 2

- 7 ounces dried soba noodles
- 2 tablespoons dried hijiki
- 1 cup green beans, trimmed and cut in half lengthwise
- 10 asparagus spears, cut the same length as the beans
- 1 teaspoon toasted sesame seeds

For the sesame dressing
- 2 tablespoons toasted sesame seeds
- 1 tablespoon light brown sugar
- 2 tablespoons soy sauce
- 1 teaspoon miso paste

This is one of my favorite combinations of tastes and textures. The sesame dressing brings all of the ingredients together, making it a satisfying one-course salad.

Bring a saucepan of water to a boil, add the noodles, and stir to separate the strands. When the water comes back to a boil and begins to rise to the top, pour in a glass of cold water and add the hijiki. Let the water return to a boil, drain, rinse under cold, running water, and set aside to drain well.

Put the beans in another saucepan of water, bring to a boil, and cook for 2–3 minutes before adding the asparagus to cook for 1 minute. Drain and refresh under cold, running water and drain well again.

To make the dressing, put the sesame seeds in a mortar, grind them to a rough texture, add the rest of the ingredients, and grind until smooth.

Put the noodles, vegetables, and the dressing in a bowl and stir to mix. Divide into two equal portions, arrange on serving dishes, garnish with the sesame seeds, and serve with chopsticks.

Mixed beans & bean sprouts with chile sesame soy dressing

This is another easy and quick recipe, using beans and bean sprouts. Serve warm in the cold season or chilled in the summer.

Cook the fava beans and carrot in a saucepan of boiling water for 2–3 minutes and drain. In a separate saucepan of boiling water, blanch the bean sprouts and drain well. Drain the canned beans and rinse under cold, running water.

Mix all the ingredients for the dressing together. Put the beans, carrot, bean sprouts, and onion in a mixing bowl, pour in the dressing, and mix well to dress. Divide the bean mixture between two serving dishes and serve either warm or chilled, with chopsticks.

Serves 2

- $\frac{1}{2}$ cup peeled fava beans, fresh or frozen
- 1 carrot, peeled and diced
- 1 cup trimmed bean sprouts
- $\frac{3}{4}$ cup canned mixed beans of your choice (drained weight)
- $\frac{1}{2}$ red onion, finely chopped

For the chile sesame soy dressing
- 2 scallions, finely minced
- 2 tablespoons soy sauce
- 1 teaspoon sesame oil
- 1 teaspoon runny honey
- 1 tablespoon toasted sesame seeds, ground
- $\frac{1}{4}$–$\frac{1}{2}$ teaspoon chile powder

Quick-pickled spring cabbage with sweet vinaigrette

Serves 2

- 4–6 large leaves of spring (or green) cabbage, roughly chopped into bite-size pieces
- 1 carrot, peeled and sliced
- 1/2 postcard-size piece of konbu, cut into thin, small strips
- 1/2 teaspoon salt
- 1/2 lotus root
- 10 snow peas, halved diagonally

For the sweet vinaigrette
- 2 tablespoons rice vinegar
- 1 tablespoon runny honey
- 1 teaspoon light soy sauce

Spring cabbages, especially pointed-head varieties, are tender and have mild sweet tastes that are best enjoyed fresh in salads. This is quite a small salad so eat it when you feel like you have eaten too much the day before.

Put the cabbage, carrot, and konbu in a bowl, sprinkle with the salt, and squeeze and mix with your hands.

Fill another bowl—which fits inside the first bowl—with water and set it on top of the cabbage mixture for 30 minutes. Cut the lotus root into halves or quarters lengthwise and slice thinly. Blanch the snow peas.

Mix all the ingredients for the sweet vinaigrette.

Squeeze the cabbage with your hands to rid it of excess water, add the snow peas and lotus root, pour in the vinaigrette, and mix well. Set the mixture aside for 10 minutes or so to let the flavor develop before serving with chopsticks.

Tip
Outside of Japan, you are likely to come across lotus root already cooked in water and sold vacuum-packed—they have a relatively long shelf life and are easy to use. If you don't use it all up, keep refrigerated in a fresh bowl of water for up to a week.

Daikon, edamame & avocado salad with yuzu vinaigrette

This is one of my favorite salads because it is not only eye-catchingly beautiful but combines so many ingredients that are all good for your health and skin.

With a Japanese mandolin, shred the daikon and carrot into a big bowl of ice-cold water. Peel and halve the cucumber lengthwise. Discard the seeds and shred like the daikon and carrot.

Slice the red onion as thinly as possible into the bowl. With your hands, gently mix the daikon, carrot, cucumber, and onion and refrigerate for at least 30 minutes while you prepare the other vegetables.

Cook the edamame in boiling water for 2 minutes, drain, cool under cold, running water, and set aside to drain further. Cut the peppers into thin julienne and discard any white fiber or seeds. Drain the daikon mixture and divide between two serving plates and scatter the peppers on top of the salad.

Halve, pit, and peel the avocado, then cut into small cubes and arrange on top of the salad. Sprinkle the edamame and pomegranate on top. Mix all the ingredients for the vinaigrette, drizzle it over the salad, and serve with chopsticks.

Serves 2

- ³/₄ daikon radish, scrubbed clean
- 1 carrot, scrubbed clean
- 1 baby cucumber
- 1 small red onion, peeled
- ²/₃ cup frozen shelled edamame
- ¹/₂ red bell pepper
- ¹/₂ yellow bell pepper
- 1 avocado
- Seeds from 1 pomegranate

For the yuzu vinaigrette
- 2 teaspoons yuzu juice (see Tip)
- 2 tablespoons rice vinegar
- 1 tablespoon light soy sauce
- 1 tablespoon runny honey

Tip
Yuzu is a yellow tangerine-like citrus fruit, of which the skin and juice are used to flavor food. Outside of Japan, the juice is sold in small bottles, which you should keep well refrigerated, once opened. If you can't find it, use lime juice instead.

Tofu, crabmeat, & avocado salad with wasabi dressing

Silky tofu and creamy avocado have a delicious affinity that is highlighted by the wasabi-based dressing. The recipe works equally well with canned tuna or cooked shrimp instead of crabmeat.

Wrap the tofu in sheets of paper towel and refrigerate for 30 minutes to drain naturally.

Soak the onion in a bowl of cold water to rid it of the smell. Cut the avocado into bite-size fan-shaped slices and drizzle with the lime juice to keep it from discoloring. Cut the tofu into bite-size pieces and arrange on a large serving platter.

Mix all the ingredients of the wasabi dressing. Drain the onion and put on top of the tofu, followed by the avocado and crabmeat. Drizzle with the wasabi dressing, garnish with parsley leaves, and serve with chopsticks.

Serves 2

- $1/2$ (12-ounce) package soft silken tofu
- $1/2$ white or red onion, thinly sliced
- 1 avocado
- juice from $1/2$ lime
- $3^1/2$ ounces lump crabmeat
- a few sprigs of flat-leaf parsley

For the wasabi dressing
- 1 teaspoon wasabi paste
- 1 tablespoon light soy sauce
- 1 tablespoon rice vinegar
- 3 tablespoons extra-virgin olive oil

Tofu Caesar salad

We all know how good and healthy tofu is, although many people think it tastes bland. But it is exactly this blandness that makes tofu an ideal ingredient to cook with other foods. Think of tofu as a white canvas, ready for you to create a delicious culinary painting.

Drain the tofu by wrapping it in sheets of paper towel and microwaving it on medium for 1 minute. Set aside to cool down and drain further while you prepare the other ingredients.

Divide and arrange the salad leaves and watercress between two dishes. Mix all the ingredients for the salad dressing and shake it well to incorporate.

Cut the tofu into 1-inch cubes. Heat the oil in a pan and fry the bacon and tofu until they become crisp. Remove the bacon and tofu with a slotted spoon to paper towels to drain, then arrange them on top of the salad leaves. Drizzle with the salad dressing, and serve with chopsticks.

Serves 2

- $1/2$ (12-ounce) package firm tofu
- 1 cup romaine lettuce leaves, roughly chopped
- $3/4$ cup watercress, trimmed
- 1 tablespoon vegetable oil
- 2 slices of streaky bacon, chopped

For the salad dressing
- $1/2$ teaspoon grated garlic
- $1/2$ tablespoon lemon juice
- $1/2$ egg yolk
- 2 anchovy fillets, finely mashed
- 2–3 drops of Worcestershire sauce
- 2 tablespoons extra-virgin olive oil
- salt and freshly ground black pepper

Tofu salad

Serves 2

- ½ (12-ounce) package firm tofu
- ½ white or red onion
- 1 baby cucumber
- 1 carrot, scrubbed clean
- 1 cup finely shredded iceberg lettuce
- 6 radishes, thinly sliced
- 1 cup watercress, washed and trimmed
- 2 teaspoons toasted sesame seeds

For the salad dressing
- 2 tablespoons toasted sesame seeds
- about a 1-inch chunk of tofu (taken from the above)
- 2 tablespoons rice vinegar
- 1 tablespoon soy sauce (preferably light soy sauce)
- 1 teaspoon sugar
- ½ teaspoon sesame oil
- 2–3 tablespoons water

In this recipe, tofu is used twice—as a main salad ingredient and as a base for the dressing.

Wrap the tofu in paper towels and microwave on medium for 1 minute to rid it of the excess water (tofu is nearly 90 percent water). Leave the tofu wrapped and let it cool down on more sheets of paper towels.

Meanwhile, slice the onion as thinly as possible and soak in cold water to refresh it and rid it of the smell. Peel the cucumber, discard the seeds, and julienne it along with the carrot.

To make the salad dressing, put the sesame seeds in a mortar and grind them to a coarse texture. Add about a 1-inch chunk of tofu and continue to grind until the mixture becomes smooth. Add the rest of the dressing ingredients and adjust the consistency with the water.

Break the tofu into bite-size pieces and divide them into two equal portions. Drain the onion slices and portion all the vegetables into two equal amounts. Arrange half the tofu pieces on a serving plate and add (in this order) lettuce, carrot, cucumber, radishes, watercress, and onion slices. Pour the dressing over the salad, garnish with the sesame seeds, and serve with chopsticks.

Japanese ceviche of plaice with grapefruit & arugula

Serves 2

- 7 ounces plaice fillet, boned and skinned
- 4 tablespoons frozen shelled edamame
- 2 big handfuls of arugula leaves
- 1 grapefruit, peeled and segmented
- 1 tablespoon extra-virgin olive oil
- 1 tablespoon light soy sauce
- 1 teaspoon mixed toasted black and white sesame seeds
- $1/2$ teaspoon chile flakes

For the ceviche marinade
- 2 tablespoons rice vinegar
- 1 teaspoon yuzu juice
- 2 limes, finely grated zest and juice

Ceviche is not Japanese. In fact, it is a speciality of the Central and South American Spanish-speaking countries. But there are similar ways of "cooking" raw fish with citrus fruits and rice vinegar in Japan.

Run your fingers over the fillet to feel if there are any bones left and pluck them out with fish tweezers as necessary. Cut the fillet in half lengthwise and slice diagonally across the grains of the flesh as thinly as possible.

To make the ceviche marinade, mix the rice vinegar, yuzu juice, and lime juice and zest in a shallow dish, and add the fish slices. Cover with plastic wrap and refrigerate to marinate for 1–1$1/2$ hours. The color of the fish should turn from translucent to opaque white as it "cooks" in the citrus marinade.

Meanwhile, cook the frozen edamame in boiling water for 2 minutes, rinse under cold, running water, drain, and set aside to drain and cool further.

Divide the arugula leaves between two serving plates and arrange the grapefruit and edamame on top. Take the fish slices out of the marinade and pat them dry with paper towels. Place and arrange them over the salad mixture. Drizzle the olive oil over the salad mound, followed by the soy sauce. Garnish with the sesame seeds and chile flakes and serve with chopsticks.

Classic salmon sashimi with daikon salad

Serves 2

- 7 ounces sashimi grade organic salmon fillet, skinless

For the daikon salad
- 1/2 large daikon radish, scrubbed clean
- 1 baby cucumber
- 1 tablespoon black sesame seeds

For wasabi and sushi ginger dressing
- 1 tablespoon sushi pickled ginger
- 1/2 teaspoon wasabi powder
- 2 tablespoons soy sauce
- 2 teaspoons rice vinegar
- 2 tablespoons water
- 1 teaspoon black sesame seeds

A cardinal principle of Japanese cuisine is that any seafood fresh enough to be eaten raw should be served raw. Why cook when you don't need to? Preparing sashimi is a highly skilled job that is probably best left to professionals. In Japan, sashimi is sold already prepared, but I am pleased to see that increasing numbers of fishmongers are selling fresh sashimi-grade seafood and are able to prepare at least a part of it. The freshness of the salmon is paramount.

You need a Japanese mandolin for this recipe, but it is an inexpensive kitchen implement that is sold in good kitchenware stores and department stores.

To make the daikon salad, using the mandolin, shred the daikon into a large bowl of ice-cold water. Peel and halve the cucumber lengthwise. Discard the seeds and shred the cucumber. Carefully mix the vegetables together and refrigerate for at least 30 minutes while you prepare the fish.

Run your fingers over the fillet to feel if any bones remain, and pluck them out with fish tweezers if necessary. Trim off any brown flesh. Slice the fillet diagonally and across the white lines of the flesh into 1/3in thick, double stamp-size rectangular pieces.

With a small blender, blend all the ingredients for the dressing until smooth. Drain the daikon and cucumber salad mixture and divide into two equal portions. Make a mound on a serving plate and garnish with black sesame seeds. Arrange the salmon pieces beside the daikon. Drizzle with the dressing and serve with chopsticks.

Salt salmon & noodle salad

In Japan, salmon is normally sold salt-cured. A little bit of salt on salmon really highlights the taste and texture. You have to think ahead to prepare this salad, I am afraid, but I am confident that you will enjoy the result.

On the night before you serve it, rub the salt all over the salmon, loosely wrap it in paper towels, place on a plate, and refrigerate overnight. The fish should feel drier and stiffer to the touch on the next day. Place the fish in a saucepan, add enough cold water to cover, and slowly bring to a low boil over a medium heat. Do not let it come to a rapid boil. Adjust the heat, simmer for 10 minutes, and remove the fish from the water to cool down.

Meanwhile, bring a saucepan of water to a boil, add the soba noodles, and stir to separate the strands. Add a glass of cold water when the water returns to a boil and begins to rise to the top. Let the water come back to a boil for a third time, drain and rinse under cold, running water, set aside to drain well, then with a pair of kitchen scissors cut the noodles into manageable lengths. Put the salad leaves and soba in a salad bowl and gently toss to distribute evenly. Mix all the ingredients for the dressing. With your hands, remove and discard the salmon skin and break the flesh into bite-size pieces. Scatter the fish pieces and scallions on the salad mixture, drizzle with the dressing, sprinkle with the sesame seeds, and serve with chopsticks.

Serves 2

- 1 teaspoon salt
- 7 ounces salmon fillet, skin on
- 7 ounces dried soba noodles
- 2 cups mixed salad leaves of your choice
- 2 scallions, finely chopped diagonally
- 2 teaspoons toasted sesame seeds, coarsely ground

For the dressing

- 2 tablespoons extra-virgin olive oil
- 2 tablespoons rice vinegar
- 1 tablespoon soy sauce
- 1 teaspoon sesame oil

Smoked salmon, daikon, & cucumber salad with watercress dressing

Smoked salmon is a wonderful ingredient; accessible and tasty, it can turn an ordinary bowl of salad into something quite special. Crisp daikon and a peppery watercress dressing beautifully counterbalance the rich oily taste and texture of the salmon.

With a mandolin, shred the daikon into a large bowl of ice-cold water. Discard the top and the bottom of the carrot and shred as you did with the daikon. Halve the cucumber lengthwise, discard the seeds, and shred. Mix the vegetables and place in the fridge for 30 minutes to crisp.

Serves 2

- 1½ daikon radishes, peeled
- 1 carrot, peeled
- 1 baby cucumber

- a handful of arugula leaves
- 3½ ounces smoked salmon, torn into manageable-length strips

For the watercress dressing
- 1 cup watercress, roughly chopped
- 2 tablespoons light soy sauce
- 2 tablespoons rice vinegar
- 1 teaspoon light brown sugar
- 1 teaspoon black sesame seeds
- 2 tablespoons sunflower oil

Meanwhile, put all the ingredients for the dressing into a blender and blend until smooth.

Drain the daikon mixture well, divide into two equal portions, and arrange on serving dishes. Put the arugula leaves on the daikon and arrange the salmon strips on top, drizzle the dressing over, and serve with chopsticks.

Scallop sashimi with daikon salad

Serves 2

For the daikon salad
- ½ large daikon radish, scrubbed clean
- 1 carrot, scrubbed clean
- 1 baby cucumber

- 4 diver scallops
- 1 scallion, finely chopped
- a few sprigs of cilantro
- 1 teaspoon mixed toasted black and white sesame seeds
- 2 teaspoons wasabi powder, mixed with 1 tablespoon water
- 2 tablespoons tamari or soy sauce

Scallops are high in protein, low in calories, and rich in vitamin B2, which helps to metabolize sugar and fat—a great diet food. I love scallops, not only for their health benefits but also for their subtle sweet taste and plump, succulent texture. They are particularly good in cold months. I urge you to try this recipe with the freshest diver scallops you can find.

With a mandolin, shred the daikon into a large bowl of ice-cold water. Discard the top and the bottom of the carrot and shred as you did with the daikon. Halve the cucumber lengthwise, discard the seeds, and shred. Mix the vegetables and place in the fridge for 30 minutes to crisp.

Clean the scallops as necessary, removing and discarding the orange or gray roe. Rinse under cold, running water and pat dry with paper towels. Slice each scallop horizontally into three pieces.

Drain the daikon salad and divide between two serving plates. Arrange 6 pieces of scallop so that they overlap one another and place them on top of each daikon salad. Scatter the scallion and cilantro leaves on top and sprinkle with the sesame seeds. To serve, make two small mounds of wasabi paste and place them on the side of each plate. Serve with small dipping dishes of tamari on the side, and chopsticks.

Squid salad with soy vinegar dressing

Serves 2

- 7 ounces squid, skin and ink sacs removed
- 2 tablespoons rice vinegar
- 2 cups red or speckled lettuce leaves
- 1 baby cucumber
- ½ red onion, thinly sliced
- a small handful of torn fresh mint leaves

For the soy vinegar dressing
- 2 tablespoons soy sauce
- 2 tablespoons rice vinegar
- 1 garlic clove, grated
- 1 teaspoon grated ginger
- 1 tablespoon runny honey
- ½–1 teaspoon finely minced red chile
- a few drops of sesame oil

Squid is a popular choice of seafood in the Japanese diet. It is well liked for its mild taste and unique texture. Nutritionally, squid contains less protein than the average fish, but it is easier to digest. It is also lower in fat and calories. However, its most notable feature is its rich taurine content (two to three times more than fish), which is an amino acid valued for lowering blood pressure and cholesterol as well as promoting a healthy liver.

Start by mixing all the ingredients for the dressing together to allow it to develop flavor.

Cut the squid bodies in half lengthwise and clean, removing any quills. Score a shallow criss-cross pattern on the inside of the squid to prevent it from curling up, taking care not to cut all the way through the flesh. Cut it into 1-inch square pieces. Cut the tentacles into bite-size pieces. Bring a saucepan of water to a boil over medium heat and add the rice vinegar. Poach the squid for 30 seconds, or until it turns opaque, and remove it with a slotted spoon.

Tear the lettuce leaves with your hands into bite-size pieces. Peel and cut the cucumber in half lengthwise and discard the seeds. Slice thinly, diagonally. Put all the squid, lettuce, cucumber, and onion in a large bowl, add the dressing, and toss to mix. Divide between two shallow dishes, garnish with the mint leaves, and serve with chopsticks.

Smoked mackerel, broccoli, green bean salad with miso sesame dressing

This salad combines multiple layers of distinct tastes and flavours and is ideally served warm in cold months. Mackerel is often undeservedly under-rated. It is a very healthy food containing high levels of unsaturated fatty acids of both eicosapentaenoic acid (EPA) and docosa-hexaenoic acid (DHA). EPA cleanses the blood and helps to prevent arteriosclerosis as well as maintaining healthy eyesight, while DHA helps to maintain healthy brain cells and helps to lower cholesterol. Mackerel is plentiful and cheap and should be eaten more often.

Serves 2

- 7 ounces smoked mackerel fillet
- 1^1/$_2$ cups broccoli florets
- 1^1/$_2$ cups cauliflower florets
- 1 carrot, scrubbed clean
- 1 cup green beans, trimmed
- 2 big handfuls of baby spinach leaves
- 2 tablespoons sunflower oil
- a few drops of sesame oil
- 2 scallions, thinly sliced
- 1 teaspoon toasted sesame seeds

For the miso sesame dressing
- 4 tablespoons toasted sesame seeds, ground
- 1 tablespoon soy sauce
- 1 teaspoon miso paste
- ^{1}/$_2$ teaspoon grated garlic
- 1 teaspoon runny honey
- 1 tablespoon rice vinegar

Run your fingers over the fleshy side of the mackerel to feel any bones and remove them using fish tweezers as necessary. Peel the skin off and, with your hands, break up the flesh into small chunks and set aside.

Cut the broccoli and cauliflower into small, bite-size pieces. Cut the carrot into chunky slices. Bring a saucepan of water to a boil and cook the broccoli, cauliflower, carrot, and beans for 2 minutes. Drain, drizzle over the oils, and cover to keep warm.

With a pestle and mortar, grind and mix together all the ingredients for the dressing. Add the spinach leaves to the vegetables and gently mix to let the spinach wilt with the heat.

Divide the vegetable mixture between two serving plates. Arrange the mackerel on top, drizzle over the dressing, and garnish with the scallions and sesame seeds. Serve with chopsticks.

Shrimp & bell pepper salad with chile soy dressing

This salad is not only beautiful on the table, it is packed with goodness to improve health and beauty. Shrimp are low in calories and fat and have high taurine content, known to lower cholesterol and blood pressure. Bell peppers have twice the vitamin C of lemon juice, which is great for beautiful skin. Peppers also have vitamin P, which helps to absorb vitamin C.

Serves 2

- ¼ small daikon radish, peeled
- 1 carrot, scrubbed clean
- 1 red or orange bell pepper
- 1 yellow bell pepper
- 7 ounces cooked, shelled medium-size shrimp
- 2 cups baby spinach leaves
- 2 teaspoons toasted sesame seeds, coarsely ground

For the chile soy dressing
- 3 tablespoons rice vinegar
- 2 tablespoons soy sauce
- 1 tablespoon runny honey
- 2 teaspoons chile sauce
- 1 teaspoon grated ginger juice
- 1 garlic clove, grated
- a few drops of sesame oil

Put all the ingredients for the dressing in a small jar with a lid and shake well to mix. Set aside to marry the flavors.

Cut both daikon and carrot into thin, 2-inch strips and soak in a bowl of cold water to refresh. Cut and deseed the peppers and thinly slice them. Drain the daikon and carrot.

Put the daikon, carrot, peppers, and shrimp in a bowl, pour on half the dressing, then toss thoroughly to evenly distribute and dress.

To assemble the salad, make a bed of spinach on two plates and place the shrimp and vegetable mix on top. Drizzle the remaining dressing over, sprinkle with the sesame seeds, and serve with chopsticks.

Tuna, avocado & spinach salad with wasabi dressing

I was highly tempted to use seared tuna steaks for this recipe, but I decided to save them for later in this book. A lunch salad recipe should be simple, quick, and easy to prepare with what you can find in your kitchen cupboard and fridge. But by no means should it be a mean affair.

Put the tuna, capers, onion, avocado, and tomato in a big mixing bowl and gently mix together.

Mix all the ingredients for the wasabi dressing together and add to the tuna mixture. Put the spinach in a separate bowl. Heat the olive oil in a small pan or stainless-steel spoon over a medium heat, then pour it over the spinach to wilt it.

Divide and place the spinach between two plates. Spoon the tuna mixture on top of the spinach beds, garnish with the scallions, top with the shredded nori, and serve with chopsticks.

Serves 2

- 6 ounces canned tuna, drained
- 1 tablespoon capers, rinsed, drained, and finely chopped
- 1/4 white or red onion, finely minced
- 1 avocado, diced
- 1 large tomato, roughly chopped
- 2 cups baby spinach leaves
- 2 tablespoons olive oil
- 2 scallions, finely chopped diagonally
- 1 sheet of nori, finely shredded

For the wasabi dressing
- 2 teaspoons wasabi powder, dissolved into 2 tablespoons water
- 1 tablespoon runny honey
- 1 tablespoon rice vinegar
- 2 tablespoons light soy sauce

Leftover chicken, cucumber, & soba noodle salad with spicy miso & sesame dressing

Serves 2

- 7 ounces dried soba noodles
- ½ cup thin green beans, trimmed
- 1 teaspoon sesame oil
- ½ white or red onion
- 1 baby cucumber, peeled
- up to 1 cup shredded leftover roast chicken
- 2–3 tablespoons pickled sushi ginger, finely shredded
- 1 cup mixed salad leaves
- 1 scallion, finely chopped diagonally
- 1 teaspoon black sesame seeds

For the spicy miso and sesame dressing
- 4 tablespoons toasted white sesame seeds, finely ground
- 1 tablespoon sugar
- 1 tablespoon light-colored miso paste
- 2 tablespoons soy sauce
- 1 tablespoon rice vinegar
- 1–2 teaspoons chile sauce (depending on your taste)

This is what I call, "Let's see what's left in the fridge for lunch." In my house, it happens quite regularly on Mondays after a family roast chicken on Sunday. The vegetables are only meant to be a guide. You can improvise with what you have in your own fridge.

Bring a saucepan of water to a boil, add the soba noodles, stir to separate the strands, and add a glass of cold water when the water comes back to a boil again and begins to rise to the top. Add the green beans and let the water return to a boil. Drain and rinse under cold, running water. Drain well again and drizzle with the sesame oil.

Slice the onion as thinly as possible and soak in cold water to refresh and rid it of the smell. Cut the cucumber into 2-inch long chunks and chop into fine matchstick pieces, but discard the seeds.

Mix all the ingredients for the spicy miso and sesame dressing.

Drain the onion slices. Put the noodles, beans, cucumber, onion, chicken, and sushi ginger in a big mixing bowl. Pour over the dressing and toss gently to coat.

Divide the salad mixture into two equal portions, arrange on serving plates, top with the salad leaves, sprinkle the chopped scallion, and sesame seeds and serve with chopsticks.

Vegetable & chicken salad with sesame miso sauce

This is a big salad lunch I love to eat on an early spring day, when the weather is not quite warm enough. As I'm sure you know, steaming the chicken and vegetables is a really healthy cooking method, with the sesame miso sauce adding that extra kick of flavour.

Cut the cabbage and chicken into bite-size pieces. Arrange the carrot, leek, and the chicken in a steaming basket. Drizzle over 2 tablespoons of sake and steam over high heat for 8 minutes.

Arrange the cabbage, broccoli, and snow peas in a separate steaming basket. Drizzle over the rest of the sake, place the basket underneath the first basket, and steam for 2–3 minutes.

Mix together all the ingredients for the sesame miso sauce and adjust the thickness with 1–2 tablespoons water.

Arrange the vegetables and chicken on a warm serving platter, drizzle over the sauce, and serve warm with chopsticks.

Serves 2

- ¼ head pointed-head green cabbage
- 2 chicken tenders
- 1 carrot, peeled and sliced diagonally
- 1 leek, trimmed and sliced diagonally
- 4 tablespoons sake
- 2 cups chopped sprouting broccoli
- 1½ cups snow peas

For the sesame miso sauce
- 3 tablespoons toasted white sesame seeds, finely ground
- 2 tablespoons light miso paste
- 1 tablespoon sugar
- 3 tablespoons rice vinegar
- 1 teaspoon grated ginger juice

Shredded chicken salad with creamy tofu dressing

Tofu is a food that never seems to stop dividing opinions. But whatever your view of tofu, this is a tasty way of using it.

Place the chicken in a saucepan and cover with plenty of water. Bring to a boil and cook for 5 minutes. Take the chicken out and let it cool down before shredding it with a fork.

Bring a separate saucepan of water to a boil. Put the tofu in a sieve and submerge in the water for 2–3 minutes. Take it out and drain. Using the same boiling water, cook the spinach for 1 minute, refresh in a bowl of cold water, and drain well.

Put the tofu in a mixing bowl and mash it to a smooth paste with the back of a spoon. Add the sesame seeds and sesame oil, mix well to combine, and season with salt and pepper. Mix in the chicken and spinach. Divide the salad mixture into two portions, transfer to two dishes, and serve with chopsticks.

Serves 2

- 2 chicken tenders
- ¼ (12-ounce) package soft silken tofu, broken into large pieces
- 2 cups spinach, roughly chopped
- 1 tablespoon toasted sesame seeds, finely ground
- 2 teaspoons sesame oil
- salt and white pepper

Beef carpaccio & eggplant with ginger dressing

Serves 2

- 1 eggplant
- 3¹/₂ ounces beef fillet
- 1 cup arugula leaves
- 1 scallion, finely chopped
- ¹/₂ teaspoon toasted sesame seeds

For the ginger soy dressing
- 2 teaspoons grated ginger juice
- ¹/₂ small garlic clove, grated
- 2 tablespoons soy sauce
- 1 tablespoon extra-virgin olive oil

This is an adaptation of a classic Italian carpaccio of beef with a Japanese twist, both in taste and the method used. I also like to try this recipe when I get hold of fresh spring lamb loin.

Preheat the broiler to the highest setting. Prick the eggplant all over and place under the broiler for about 20 minutes to brown the skin and cook the eggplant flesh. Slice the beef fillet into strips, as thinly as possible. Take a length of plastic wrap, about 24 inches long, and fold it over. Place a slice of the beef about one third of the way from the left-hand side of the plastic wrap, fold it over the beef to cover, and with a rolling pin gently smash the meat, working from the center to out, until wafer thin.

Mix together all the ingredients for the ginger soy dressing. Peel off the eggplant skin, roughly chop the eggplant flesh, and divide into two equal portions. Make mounds of eggplant in the center of two plates. Arrange the beef slices around the mounds, put the arugula leaves on top, drizzle with the dressing, garnish with the scallion and sesame seeds, and serve with chopsticks.

Beef, arugula & grapefruit with wasabi dressing

Serves 2

- 4 ounces beef sirloin or fillet
- ¹/₂ teaspoon sesame oil
- 2 tablespoons rice vinegar
- 2 cups arugula leaves
- 1 grapefruit, peeled and segmented
- 1 tablespoon toasted sesame seeds

For the wasabi dressing
- 1 teaspoon wasabi powder, mixed with 1 teaspoon water
- 1 tablespoon runny honey
- 2 tablespoons rice vinegar
- 2 tablespoons light soy sauce

This classical way of cooking meat or fish is called tataki, which means to beat or hit—you slap the meat with the palm of your hand to flatten and tenderize it. Choose as good quality beef as you can get for the best result.

Take the beef out of the fridge and let it come to room temperature, because cold meat is tough and takes longer to cook. Trim off any fat. Put a heavy frying pan over high heat. Pat the beef dry with paper towels, brush with the sesame oil, and brown for 1–2 minutes on each side, depending on the thickness of the meat and your preference. Transfer the meat to a cutting board, sprinkle the rice vinegar over it, and let it rest.

Meanwhile, put the arugula leaves on two serving plates with the grapefruit segments arranged around them. Mix all the ingredients for the dressing. With a sharp knife, cut the meat into thin slices. Separate the slices and give each a light but firm slap with the palm of your hand. Arrange the beef slices on top of the salad, drizzle with the dressing, sprinkle with the sesame seeds, and serve with chopsticks.

Crisp duck with orange & watercress salad

The key to achieving a really crisp duck skin is to ensure that the skin is dry before cooking, so take the breast out of its wrapping in advance. Duck is often seen as fatty but in this recipe most of the fat is drained off to make the crisp skin and we use only one breast to make two servings. So enjoy this delicious salad with a clear conscience!

Serves 2

- 1 duck breast
- $^1/_2$ teaspoon salt
- 1 orange or blood orange
- 2 cups watercress

For the dressing

- 2 tablespoons orange juice
- 1 tablespoon soy sauce
- 2 teaspoons rice vinegar
- 2 teaspoons wasabi powder

With a fork, prick the duck breast, rub the salt onto the skin, and set aside to draw out the moisture. Grate the orange for its zest, peel, and separate the segments, carefully removing all the membranes.

Heat a heavy frying pan over a medium heat, place the duck skin side down, and cook for 5 minutes to render the fat. Remove the duck and pour off any fat, return the pan to the heat, and turn up the heat to high. Put the duck back in the pan skin side up for 2 minutes to seal and turn it over on the skin side for 3–5 minutes, or until the skin is crisp and golden. Remove the duck to a plate lined with paper towels, skin side up, to rest.

Mix all the ingredients for the dressing with the orange zest. Divide and arrange the watercress and orange segments on two serving plates. Cut the duck into thin slices and arrange them over the salad mixture, drizzle over the dressing, and serve with chopsticks.

The simplest and most quintessential Japanese meal is rice with a bowl of soup and a few slices of pickled vegetables. In Japanese cuisine, soups are the most important side dish to accompany rice; in fact, in a formal meal with several courses, both clear broth-based and miso-flavored soups are served at both ends of the meal. Miso-based soups with a variety of seasonal ingredients make a quick and easy, healthy one-bowl meal. Despite the growing Westernization of eating habits, millions of Japanese still begin their day with a bowl of miso soup for breakfast and finish it with another bowl at the end of the day.

Miso is made of fermented soybeans and other grains such as rice, wheat, and barley. The color of miso ranges from pale cream to steely, dark brown and the color is a rough indication of taste—the lighter the color, the less salty the taste. But this is a rather simplistic generalization and doesn't begin to describe the rich and complex tastes, flavors, and aromas of miso. Miso is a very healthy food—the soybean's high-quality protein is converted into easily digestible amino acid. Miso helps to lower cholesterol and blood pressure; it is also anticancerous, antioxidant, and anti-aging. Although by no means conclusive, much research shows that Japanese women suffer no or fewer menopausal symptoms, linked, it is believed, to their higher intake of soy protein such as tofu and miso. Recent research has revealed that soybeans contain several phenolic compounds called isoflavones that resemble the human estrogen hormone and provide similar health benefits.

Remember, soups are also eaten with chopsticks in Japan. Eat the meat and vegetables with chopsticks and then pick up the bowl with both hands to drink the soup.

Soups

Dashi

A good bowl of soup starts with delicious dashi—Japanese stock. Compared to its Western counterpart, dashi is a quick and easy-to-prepare stock. The quality of dashi is particularly important for miso soups in which miso is almost the sole seasoning ingredient. I have listed four methods of making dashi at the beginning of this section.

Primary dashi

- 2 postcard-size pieces of konbu, wiped clean, with incisions made into them
- 2½ cups water
- 5 packets dried bonito fish flakes

This is a finely balanced dashi that is most suitable for clear soups and miso soups with vegetables with delicate aromas.

Place the konbu in a saucepan with the water and let it infuse for 20 minutes. Heat the saucepan over a medium heat, taking care not to let it reach a boil, and remove the konbu pieces when they begin to float to the top; bring to a full boil. Add the bonito fish flakes. There is no need to stir. Immediately turn off the heat and let the fish flakes settle at the bottom. Filter through a cheesecloth-lined sieve. Reserve the bonito flakes and konbu for making Secondary Dashi (see below).

Secondary dashi

- reserved konbu and bonito fish flakes from the Primary Dashi (see above)
- 1 packet dried bonito fish flakes
- 2½ cups water

While Primary Dashi is best suited to clear soups by virtue of its aroma, delicate flavor, and clarity, Secondary Dashi, with its more robust taste, makes a good base for miso soups with seafood or root vegetables.

Put the reserved konbu and fish flakes, along with the fresh fish flakes, in a saucepan with the water and heat over medium heat. Remove the konbu when the water begins to boil and continue to cook until the water is reduced by 10 percent. Filter through a cheesecloth-lined sieve.

Vegetarian dashi

- 2 postcard-size pieces of konbu, wiped clean, with incisions made into them
- 3 dried shiitake mushrooms
- 4¼ cups water, boiled and cooled

Here is a vegetarian version of dashi that is very subtle and suitable for gentle vegetable soups.

Put all the ingredients together in a bowl with the water and set aside to infuse at a room temperature for 3–4 hours in cooler months, or 2–3 hours in the summer. The dashi will keep up to a week, refrigerated.

Anchovy dashi

- 1 ounce dried anchovies, heads and entrails removed, halved lengthwise
- 2 postcard-size pieces of konbu, wiped clean, with incisions made into them
- 2$\frac{1}{2}$ cups water

This is a type of fish stock made with very small, silvery, sun-dried anchovies. Savory anchovy dashi is much stronger than primary or secondary dashi, made with bonito fish flakes, and it makes a very tasty base for thick and rich miso soups.

Put the prepared anchovies and the konbu in a saucepan with the water and let it infuse for 20 minutes. Put the saucepan over a medium heat and slowly bring to just under a boil while removing any foam from the surface and cook for 5–6 minutes. Turn off the heat and filter through a cheesecloth-lined sieve.

Water dashi

- 2 postcard-size pieces of konbu, with incisions made into them
- 1 ounce dried anchovies, heads and entrails removed
- 2 dried shiitake mushrooms
- 4$\frac{1}{4}$ cups water, boiled, cooled

With no cooking involved, this is by far the easiest method for making a reliable, basic dashi.

Put all the ingredients together in a lidded jar and refrigerate overnight. The dashi will keep for up to a week, refrigerated.

Dashi no moto
(instant dashi powder)

This is a dry granular form of dashi widely used in Japanese kitchens nowadays. Think of it as a Japanese equivalent of a boullion cube; in other words, a convenient pantry standby that should be used sparingly.

Miso

Tips for making a good miso soup

To enjoy miso's rich and complex tastes and unique flavor, never boil it for a long time. Add it only when all the other ingredients in the soup are cooked through and let the soup return to a boil only for 1 second before turning off the heat. A rough guide to the amount of miso paste per person is between 1 tablespoon and a heaping tablespoon.

You can enrich and deepen the flavors of miso soup by blending two or three different varieties of miso paste. Use paler and less salty ones to create comforting blends in colder months and use darker varieties to make a refreshing flavor in the summer. You can create your own favorite blends by experimenting and combining different varieties of miso pastes. Do not put a wad of miso paste directly into the soup and expect it to dissolve on its own. Always use a ladleful of the soup liquid to soften the paste in a small bowl first or use a small, fine-mesh sieve and the back of a wooden spoon to push it through into the soup.

Chilled miso soup of eggplant, tomato, edamame, & cucumber

For those who think that miso soup is always served hot, here is a refreshing, chilled miso soup to enjoy during the summer. I suggest serving it in a chilled glass bowl. Eggplant is low in calories and helps to reduce cholesterol. It also contains polyphenol, found in red wine, too, which helps to lower blood pressure, and is anti-aging and anticancerous. Although eggplants are available throughout the year, they are at their best in the summer and early autumn.

Serves 2

- 1 medium eggplant
- 6 vine-ripened cherry tomatoes
- 1 tablespoon vegetable oil, for brushing
- 2 tablespoons frozen shelled edamame
- 1¼ cups Dashi (pages 106–107)—primary, water, or vegetarian
- 1 baby cucumber, thinly sliced
- 2 tablespoons light-colored miso paste
- 1 shallot, peeled and thinly sliced
- a small handful of flat-leaf parsley

Preheat a heavy, cast-iron grill pan to high. Cut off and discard the stem of the eggplant, halve it lengthwise, and slice diagonally into thick chunks. Brush the eggplant and tomatoes with the oil and place on the hot pan to brown the surfaces. At the same time, cook the edamame in a small saucepan of boiling water for 2 minutes, then drain and set aside.

Put the eggplant in a saucepan with the dashi. Place over medium heat to cook for 5 minutes, taking care not to let it come to a boil. Add the tomatoes, edamame, and cucumber. Cook for 2 minutes longer.

Put the miso paste in a small bowl and add a ladleful of the soup liquid to dilute it. Pour it into the saucepan. Turn up the heat and let the soup come to a boil for 1 second, then quickly turn off the heat. Let the soup cool to room temperature, before refrigerating it for 1 hour.

Soak the shallot slices in a bowl of cold water to rid them of their smell. Drain. Stir the soup and ladle it into two chilled bowls. Arrange the shallot on top, garnish with the parsley, and serve with chopsticks.

Chilled misopacho

Serves 2

- 1 baby cucumber, peeled, seeded, and roughly chopped
- 2 large, very ripe tomatoes, roughly chopped
- ½ small red onion, roughly chopped
- ¼–½ large red chile, stemmed and deseeded
- 2 teaspoons chopped ginger
- 1 garlic clove
- ½ cup tomato juice
- juice of 1 lime
- 2 tablespoons rice vinegar
- 2 tablespoons soy sauce
- 1 tablespoon plus 2 teaspoons extra-virgin olive oil
- 1 tablespoon red miso paste
- salt and freshly ground pepper
- 6 vine-ripened cherry tomatoes, halved
- 1 celery stalk, strings removed and diced
- a few sprigs of cilantro

I first came across gazpacho over three decades ago now. I instantly fell in love with it and have been making it ever since. This is my latest version, with a few Japanese twists. Miso paste brings an extra depth of flavor to the soup, without overpowering it.

Put the cucumber, chopped tomatoes, onion, chile, ginger, and garlic in a food processor or blender to purée. Add the tomato juice, lime juice, rice vinegar, soy sauce, 1 tablespoon of the oil, and the miso paste. Purée until smooth and well blended. Adjust the seasoning.

Transfer to a large bowl, cover with plastic wrap, and refrigerate for at least 4 hours, but preferably overnight, to allow the flavors to fully develop.

Divide the soup between two chilled bowls, top with the cherry tomatoes and diced celery. Drizzle with the remaining olive oil and garnish with cilantro. Serve chilled with chopsticks.

Grilled eggplant & bell pepper miso soup with ginger mustard

Ginger has long been used in traditional Chinese medicine as well as a popular ingredient in all Asian cooking. It is a natural sterilizer, increases the body's metabolism, aids digestion, and encourages perspiration. And furthermore, recent findings show that ginger also helps to reduce cholesterol and lowers blood pressure.

Preheat the broiler. Prick the eggplant all over. Line a baking sheet with aluminum foil and place the eggplant on it to broil for 15 minutes. Turn it over to brown the other side.

Chop the peppers into bite-size pieces and brush with the oil. Add the peppers to the eggplant and grill for 10–15 minutes longer, or until the eggplant is browned all over and the peppers are cooked.

Meanwhile, mix the grated ginger with the mustard and set aside to develop flavor. Transfer the eggplant to a plate and with a bamboo skewer, peel off the skin; cut into bite-size pieces. Divide the vegetables between two bowls.

Put the dashi in a saucepan and bring to a boil over medium heat. Put both of the miso pastes in a small bowl and ladle in some of the dashi to soften and dilute. Pour it back into the saucepan. Turn up the heat to let the soup come to a boil for 1 second. Ladle into the two bowls and top with a dab of ginger mustard. Serve with chopsticks.

Serves 2

- 1 medium eggplant
- $^1/_2$ red bell pepper
- $^1/_2$ yellow bell pepper
- $^1/_2$ green bell pepper
- $^1/_2$ tablespoon vegetable oil
- 2 teaspoons grated ginger
- $^1/_2$ tablespoon dry mustard powder
- 1$^1/_4$ cups Dashi (pages 106–107)— primary, water, or vegetarian
- 1 tablespoon medium-colored miso paste
- 1 tablespoon red- or dark-colored miso paste

Japanese mushroom miso soup

Serves 2

- 7 ounces Japanese mushrooms such as shiitake, shimeji, enoki, and maitake, choosing at least two different varieties (see Tips)
- 1½ cups Dashi (pages 106–107)—primary, water, or vegetarian
- 1 tablespoon light-colored miso paste
- 1 tablespoon medium-colored miso paste
- 1 tablespoon wakame, softened in water and drained
- 2 scallions, finely chopped diagonally

The mild, warm, and moist climate of the Japanese archipelago makes it a treasure house for mushrooms of all varieties, and Japanese people love mushrooms. Mushrooms have vitamin D, which helps the body to absorb calcium, and vitamin B2, otherwise called the beauty vitamin because it metabolizes fat and sugar as well as lowering cholesterol levels in the blood. Above all, mushrooms are a low-calorie food, so enjoy this virtually fat-free soup.

Put the mushrooms in a saucepan with the dashi and bring them to a boil over medium heat.

Put the miso pastes in a small bowl, ladle in some of the dashi to soften and dilute the pastes, then pour back into the saucepan. Add the wakame. Turn up the heat and let it come to a boil for just 1 second. Ladle into two bowls, garnish with the scallions, and serve immediately with chopsticks.

Tips

Depending on which mushrooms you choose, here are some tips for preparing them to make bite-size pieces. For shiitake, discard the stems and slice the caps. When preparing shimeji and enoki mushrooms, discard the bases of both; separate the mushrooms with your hands. For maitake mushrooms, discard the bases and tear the delicate, lacework-like mushrooms into manageable pieces with your hands.

Creamy roast pumpkin miso soup

Serves 2

- 1 pound buttercup (green-skinned) pumpkin
- 1 tablespoon vegetable oil, for brushing
- $1/2$ teaspoon salt
- 1 teaspoon grated ginger
- $1^1/4$ cups Dashi (pages 106–107)—primary, water, or vegetarian
- 2 tablespoons white- or light-colored miso paste
- 1 teaspoon toasted black and white sesame seeds

Pumpkin is a very healthy vegetable. It is rich in beta-carotene, which becomes vitamin A once digested, and it strengthens the skin's mucous membrane to protect the body from infectious diseases. Pumpkin also contains twice as much vitamin C as tomatoes and has one of the highest vitamin E contents. Vitamin E is an effective antioxidant and helps to slow down the ageing process. Roasting draws out the delicious, natural sweetness of pumpkins. I'm going to allow you to eat this one with a spoon! But remember to take your time to eat and appreciate this health-giving soup.

Preheat the oven to 200°C/400°F/Gas Mark 6. Cut the pumpkin into four wedges. Remove the seeds, brush with the oil, sprinkle with the salt, and place in a roasting pan, skin side down, to roast for 45 minutes or until very tender.

Scoop the flesh from the skin and put it in a saucepan. Mash until very smooth. Add the ginger and the dashi and stir until combined. Place the saucepan over high heat and bring to a boil.

Put the miso paste in a small bowl and ladle in a small amount of the soup liquid to dilute the paste. Pour it back into the saucepan and turn up the heat to let it come to a boil for 1 second. Ladle into two bowls, sprinkle with the sesame seeds, and serve immediately.

Spinach & burdock miso soup with maitake mushrooms

Serves 2

- 1 small burdock root, scrubbed clean
- about 2 ounces maitake mushrooms
- 2 cups spinach, washed and drained
- 1¼ cups Dashi (pages 106–107)—primary, secondary, water, or vegetarian
- 1 tablespoon light-colored miso paste
- 1 tablespoon medium-colored or red miso paste
- 1 teaspoon toasted sesame seeds

The Japanese are the only nation to eat burdock, a long and slim root vegetable. The burdock's main component is a non-digestible carbohydrate, which creates the feeling of being satisfied, and also provides a unique, crisp texture and flavor. Recent research shows that the lignin that is found just under the surface is anticancerous, discharges cholesterols, and prevents arteriosclerosis and diabetes. Therefore, clean them by scraping off the outer layer of skin rather than peeling off the entire skin. Burdock is a healthy ally for dieters. Bags of frozen sliced burdock are available at Japanese grocery stores.

In order to maximize the surface area of the burdock and preserve its unique flavor, shave it with a knife as if you are sharpening a pencil. Soak in water for 10–15 minutes and drain well. Cut and discard the base of the maitake mushrooms and tear into bite-size pieces with your hands.

Chop the spinach into 2-inch lengths. Put the burdock in a saucepan with the dashi and bring to a boil over medium heat. Adjust the heat to simmer for 5 minutes. Add the maitake and spinach and cook for 3 minutes.

Put the miso pastes in a small bowl and ladle in a small amount of the soup liquid to soften and dilute the pastes. Pour it back into the saucepan and turn up the heat to let it come to a boil for 1 second. Ladle the soup into two warm bowls, sprinkle with the sesame seeds, and serve immediately with chopsticks.

Japanese corn chowder

Sweet white miso lends an exotic flavor to freshly crushed corn—a tasty marriage of East and West. I suggest serving this chilled on warm Indian-summer days, or piping hot on dull and gray autumn days to provide comfort for both the body and the soul.

Serves 2

- ½ (12-ounce) package soft silken tofu
- 1 fresh corn on the cob
- pinch of salt
- 1 teaspoon grated ginger
- 1¼ cups Dashi (pages 106–107)—primary, secondary, water, or vegetarian
- 2 tablespoons mirin
- 2 tablespoons white miso paste
- ½ tablespoon sesame oil
- a few sprigs of fresh cilantro, roughly chopped

Wrap the tofu in sheets of paper towel and let it drain on a slightly tilted cutting board for 20–30 minutes. If you are short of time, place a plate with a little weight on top of the tofu to speed up the draining. Or, if you are really pressed, microwave on medium for 1 minute.

Cook the corn, covered, in lightly salted boiling water for 10–12 minutes, then cut the kernels from the cob. Put the corn in a food processor or blender and blend until coarsely chopped. Add the tofu and the ginger to blend until the mixture is uniformly smooth.

Put the corn mixture in a saucepan together with the dashi and mirin, over high heat and bring to a boil. Reduce the heat to simmer for 5 minutes.

Put the miso paste in a small bowl and ladle in a small amount of the soup liquid to soften and dilute the paste. Pour it back into the saucepan and turn up the heat to let it come to a boil for 1 second. Adjust the seasoning with salt, if necessary. Ladle the soup into two bowls and drizzle with the sesame oil. Garnish with the cilantro and serve with chopsticks.

Tofu, seaweed, carrot, leek, & sprouting broccoli miso soup

Serves 2

- ¼ (12-ounce) package firm tofu
- 2 tablespoons dried wakame
- 1¼ cups Dashi (pages 106–107)—secondary, water, or vegetarian
- 1 small carrot, peeled and sliced diagonally
- 1 leek, trimmed and sliced diagonally
- 5 ounces sprouting broccoli, cut diagonally
- 1 heaping tablespoon light-colored miso paste
- 1 heaping tablespoon medium-colored miso paste
- 1 teaspoon toasted sesame seeds, coarsely ground

This is a variation on a classic miso soup with tofu and wakame seaweed. A miso soup is generally made with two or three ingredients, but I have added a few more late-winter/early-spring vegetables to create a nourishing soup.

Wrap the tofu in sheets of paper towel and let it drain on a slightly tilted cutting board for 20–30 minutes. If you are short of time, place a plate with a little weight on top of the tofu to speed up the draining. Or, if you are really pressed, microwave on medium for 1 minute.

Meanwhile, to soften the wakame, soak it in a bowl of cold water for 10 minutes and drain. With the dashi, put the carrot and leek in a saucepan and heat it over medium heat but make sure it does not reach a full boil. Simmer for 5 minutes.

Cut the tofu into dice-size pieces; add the tofu, wakame, and broccoli to the saucepan. Cook for 3 minutes. Put the miso pastes in a small bowl and ladle in a small amount of the soup liquid to dilute the pastes. Pour it back into the saucepan and turn up the heat to let it come to a boil for 1 second. Ladle the soup into two bowls, garnish with the sesame seeds, and serve with chopsticks.

Caramelized onion miso soup with burnt tofu

Serves 2

- ¼ (12-ounce) package burnt tofu (see Tip) or firm tofu
- 1 tablespoon vegetable oil
- 4 red onions, thinly sliced
- 4 tablespoons black rice vinegar or red wine vinegar
- 1 teaspoon sugar
- 1 tablespoon soy sauce
- 1¼ cups Dashi (pages 106–107)—secondary, water, or vegetarian
- 1 tablespoon light-colored miso paste
- 1 tablespoon red or medium-colored miso paste

This is the Japanese answer to the famous French onion soup. The secret to creating a deep-flavored sweetness is to sauté the onion with lots of patience.

Whether you have burnt or normal, firm tofu, it needs to be well drained. Wrap the tofu in sheets of paper towel and let it drain on a slightly angled cutting board for 20 minutes. Dice the tofu and set aside.

Put the oil in a saucepan and sauté the onions for 15 minutes over low heat, stirring constantly to prevent them browning. Add the vinegar, sugar, and soy sauce and continue to cook until the liquid is reduced to almost nothing. Pour in the dashi and increase the heat to high to bring to a boil.

Put the miso pastes in a small bowl and ladle in a small amount of the soup liquid to soften and dilute the pastes. Pour it back into the saucepan and turn up the heat to let it come to a boil for 1 second. Ladle into two bowls, top with the tofu, and serve immediately with chopsticks.

Tip

Burnt tofu is firm cotton tofu that is scorched on the surface. If you are unable to find it, use a well-drained, firm tofu and broil or burn it with a food torch.

Leek and turnip miso soup with chicken

Serves 2

- 2 boneless chicken thighs, skin on
- 1¼ cups Dashi (pages 106–107)—secondary or water
- 1 medium leek, trimmed and sliced
- 1 turnip, peeled and cut into bite-size wedges
- 1 medium carrot, peeled and cut into thick slices
- 2 tablespoons white- or light-colored miso paste

You will love this delicious combination of leek and turnip, two lovely winter vegetables that are sure to keep the cold at bay in the winter. Crisp chicken skin creates a tasty, contrasting texture, without adding too many calories to the bowl.

Peel the skin off the chicken and reserve it; cut the flesh into bite-size pieces. Blanch the skin in boiling water, pat it dry, and slice into thin strips. Put the chicken with the dashi in a saucepan and bring to a boil over medium heat. Reduce the heat to simmer for 5 minutes.

Meanwhile, sauté the chicken skin in a small frying pan without any oil until it becomes crisp and set aside on paper towels to soak up any oil. Add the vegetables to the chicken dashi broth and simmer for another 5 minutes or until the vegetables are cooked through.

Put the miso paste in a small bowl and ladle in a small amount of the soup liquid to soften and dilute the paste. Pour it back into the saucepan and turn up the heat to let it come to a boil for 1 second. Ladle the soup into two warm bowls, top with the crisp skin, and serve immediately with chopsticks.

Pork miso soup with konnyaku

Serves 2

- 1 block of konnyaku
- 1 tablespoon sesame oil
- 2 ounces pork belly, thinly sliced
- about 1-inch piece of ginger, roughly chopped
- 1 carrot, peeled and roughly chopped
- 1 medium parsnip, peeled and roughly chopped
- 1¼ cups Dashi (pages 106–107)—secondary, water, or vegetarian
- 6 snow peas, cut in half diagonally
- 1 tablespoon light soy sauce
- 1 tablespoon red or medium-colored miso paste
- 1 tablespoon light-colored miso paste
- 1 tablespoon pickled sushi ginger, roughly chopped
- 1 teaspoon toasted sesame seeds

Konnyaku means "the devil's tongue" or "elephant foot" in Japanese. Despite its unappealing name, it is a dieter's dream food. This speckled, gray, gelatinous and elastic block is made from the root of the konnyaku plant. It has no fat, no calories, and little taste. It works like a cleansing agent to rid the digestive system of cholesterols, impurities, and waste matter. It is sold vacuum-packed with a little limewater. Combining konnyaku with meat is an effective way to reduce cholesterol.

With your hands, break the konnyaku into small bite-size pieces. Put the sesame oil in a saucepan, place it over medium heat, and sauté the pork for 3 minutes. Add the ginger, carrot, parsnip, and konnyaku. Cook for 3 minutes longer.

Add the dashi and snow peas and bring to a boil, scooping off any foam that floats to the surface. Reduce the heat to maintain a simmering temperature. Season with the soy sauce. Put the miso pastes in a small bowl and ladle in a small amount of the soup liquid to soften and dilute the pastes. Pour it back into the saucepan and turn up the heat to let it come to a boil for 1 second. Ladle the soup into two bowls and top with the sushi ginger. Sprinkle with the sesame seeds and serve immediately with chopsticks.

Asparagus, pea, & new potato miso soup with salmon

Asparagus, new potatoes, and peas all signal the beginning of summer. I like to eat them as much as possible during their all-too-short season. This recipe gives an unusual but delicious way of enjoying all those wonderful seasonal offerings.

Preheat the broiler to high. Brush the salmon with the oil and season with salt and pepper. Place the salmon on a broiling rack skin side down and broil for 5 minutes or until the flesh of the fish is browned. Take the fish out of the grill and let it cool down until it is cool enough to handle. Remove the skin and and break the fish into bite-size chunks with your hands.

Serves 2

- 3^1/$_2$ ounces salmon fillet
- a few drops of vegetable oil, for brushing
- pinch of salt and freshly ground black pepper
- 2–4 new potatoes, scrubbed clean and thickly sliced
- 1^1/$_4$ cups Dashi (pages 106–107)—secondary or water
- ^{1}/$_2$ cup fresh peas
- 6 asparagus spears, chopped diagonally
- 1 tablespoon light-colored miso paste
- 1 tablespoon medium-colored miso paste
- a small handful of pea shoots, to garnish (optional)

Put the potatoes in a saucepan with the dashi to cook over medium heat for 5 minutes, adjusting the heat, if necessary, so that the dashi does not reach boiling point. Add the peas, asparagus, and salmon and continue to cook for 3 minutes.

Put the miso pastes in a small bowl and ladle in a small amount of the soup liquid to soften and dilute the pastes. Pour it back into the saucepan and turn up the heat to let it come to a boil for 1 second. Ladle the soup into two bowls, garnish with pea shoots, if using, and serve immediately with chopsticks.

Clam chowder miso soup with crisp deep-fried tofu

This is a classic, creamy clam chowder with a Japanese twist.

Microwave the deep-fried tofu for 30 seconds on medium to rid it of any excess oil. Cut it into stamp-size pieces. Dry-toast the deep-fried tofu in a small non-stick frying pan over medium heat, shaking the pan regularly for 3–5 minutes or until the tofu becomes crisp. Transfer to paper towels and set aside until needed.

Serves 2

- 1 sheet of deep-fried tofu, defrosted if frozen
- 1 tablespoon vegetable oil
- 1 small red onion, finely minced
- 1 celery stalk, finely chopped
- 2–4 new potatoes, scrubbed clean and roughly diced
- 1 (6$^{1}/_{2}$-ounce) can clams, drained
- 1$^{1}/_{4}$ cups Dashi (pages 106–107)—secondary, water, or anchovy
- $^{1}/_{2}$ cup soymilk
- $^{1}/_{2}$ teaspoon agar agar, diluted in 2 teaspoons water
- 2 tablespoons light-colored miso paste
- 1 scallion, finely chopped diagonally
- 1 teaspoon toasted sesame seeds

Put the oil in a large sauté pan, place over medium heat, and sweat the onion for 3 minutes. Add the celery and potatoes to sauté for 3 minutes. Add the clams and continue to sauté for 2–3 minutes before adding half of the dashi.

Transfer the soup mixture to a blender or food processor to blend—working in small batches, if necessary. Return the soup to the saucepan and add the remainder of the dashi and the soymilk. Place the saucepan over medium heat to bring it just to a simmer. Adjust the heat so that the soup does not boil but remains just below a boil. Simmer for 5 minutes.

Add the agar agar to thicken the soup. Put the miso paste in a small bowl, ladle in a small amount of the soup liquid to soften and dilute the paste. Pour it back into the saucepan and turn up the heat to let it come to a boil for 1 second. Ladle the soup into two bowls. Garnish with the crisp deep-fried tofu, scallion, and sesame seeds and serve with chopsticks.

Shrimp & tomato miso soup with okra

Serves 2

- 6 medium-size fresh head-on shrimp
- 1$\frac{1}{4}$ cups Dashi (pages 106–107)—secondary or water
- 2 large vine-ripened tomatoes
- 1 tablespoon dark-colored miso paste
- 1 tablespoon red miso paste
- 6 okra pods, blanched, stems discarded and chopped into $\frac{1}{6}$ inch thick slices

This is a visually stunning soup with an unusual marriage of ingredients that complement each other really well.

Remove the heads from the shrimp and shell the tails. Make a shallow slit along the back of the shrimp tails to remove the veins. Put the heads and shells of the shrimp in a saucepan with the dashi over medium heat. Adjust the heat, if necessary, to ensure that the dashi continues to simmer just below the boiling point.

Meanwhile, cut a slit around the middle of each tomato. To remove the tomato skins, put them in boiling water for a few minutes. Blanch the okra in the same water. Peel off the tomato skins. Cut in half horizontally to remove the seeds and chop into bite-size pieces.

With a slotted spoon, remove and discard the shrimp heads and shells from the dashi. Add the shrimp tails to cook for 3 minutes or until they turn pink and are cooked.

Put the miso pastes in a small bowl and add a ladleful of the dashi to soften and dilute the pastes. Pour the miso back into the saucepan. Turn up the heat to let the soup boil for 1 second and then add the tomatoes and okra. Ladle into two bowls and serve with chopsticks.

Let's be totally honest . . . how many times have you regretted eating a heavy dinner late in the evening, knowing that what you have just eaten will be an unspent energy source and may well cause you a disturbed night of sleep? A large evening meal is a particularly bad idea if you are trying to lose weight. But I have done this count- less times because, apart from holidays and weekends, evenings are often the only time of day when I can really take time to enjoy cooking and relax together with my family and friends.

In this section, I have come up with delicious, low-calorie and low-fat, easy to digest yet satisfying and comforting recipes to wind down the day, guaranteed to give you a good night's beauty sleep.

Light suppers

How to prepare sushi rice

Serves 2

- 1 cup Japanese-style short-grain rice
- scant 1 cup water
- 1 postcard-size piece of konbu

For the sushi vinegar mix
- 2 tablespoons rice vinegar
- 1 tablespoon sugar
- 1 teaspoon salt

Put the rice in a bowl, cover with cold water, and stir quickly with your hands until the water becomes milky-white and then pour the water away. Repeat the process until the water runs clear.

Transfer the rice to a sieve and set it aside for at least 30 minutes or, ideally, for 1 hour. The resting is particularly important when preparing sushi rice because it allows the rice to absorb the moisture and plump up.

Put the rice in a tight-lidded, heavy-bottom saucepan—a small Le Creuset one is ideal. Add the water and the konbu, cover with the lid, and bring to a boil over medium-low heat.

Do not lift the lid but look out for thin wisps of steam escaping and listen for the bubbling sound. Increase the heat to high and cook for 3 minutes. Turn off the heat. Again, do not lift the lid; let it stand to steam for 10–15 minutes.

For the sushi vinegar, mix all the ingredients for the sushi vinegar mixture in a non-metallic bowl and stir until all the sugar and salt are dissolved.

Discard the konbu and transfer the cooked rice to a moistened, shallow, flat-based basin. Sprinkle the sushi vinegar over the rice, and with a wooden spatula in a sideways cutting motion, toss the rice to coat with the vinegar until all the vinegar has been absorbed and the rice becomes glossy.

Fan the rice to cool while tossing—this is easier if you have someone else to stand by. (The job is traditionally given to a young apprentice in a sushi restaurant in Japan.) If you are not using the rice immediately, cover with a clean, damp cloth and eat on the same day. Sushi rice can be prepared up to 3 hours in advance but do not refrigerate.

Eggplant & broccoli sushi

Serves 2

- 1 medium eggplant
- salt
- 6 broccoli florets, trimmed
- 1¼ cups prepared sushi rice (see opposite)
- 2 tablespoons pickled sushi ginger, finely chopped
- 1 tablespoon toasted sesame seeds

Eggplant is almost calorie-free, and the sponge-like flesh absorbs any taste or flavor you may wish to create—another great diet food. Although there are no particularly noteworthy nutrients, polyphenol, which gives the eggplant its vibrant color, is known to be an antioxidant which helps to slow down the aging process.

Cut the eggplant into quarters lengthwise and then cut them diagonally into bite-size, diamond-shaped pieces. Bring a saucepan of salted water to a boil and blanch the eggplant for 2 minutes. Drain in a sieve and sprinkle with a pinch of salt to revive the color. At the same time, bring another saucepan of salted water to a boil, blanch the broccoli, and drain. Put the sushi rice and the ginger in a bowl and mix to incorporate.

Divide the sushi rice mixture between two serving dishes and arrange the eggplant and broccoli on top, garnish with the sesame seeds, and serve with chopsticks.

Bamboo shoot sushi

Serves 2

- 1 (8-ounce) can sliced bamboo shoots, or 100g vacuum-packed bamboo shoots
- ½ deep-fried tofu pouch
- 1 boneless chicken thigh
- about ¾ cup Dashi (page 106)
- 2 tablespoons soy sauce
- 2 tablespoons mirin
- 1¼ cups prepared sushi rice (see opposite)
- a small handful of shredded nori
- 1 tablespoon pickled sushi ginger, finely shredded

Bamboo shoots are high in edible fiber, which makes them great allies for dieters. Outside Japan, bamboo shoots are sold ready-prepared in cans or water-filled vacuum packs.

Drain the bamboo shoots, rinse briefly with water, pat dry, and cut into bite-size pieces if necessary. Put the tofu pouch in a sieve and pour boiling water over it to remove any excess oil. Pat dry and slice into small strips.

Remove and discard the skin of the chicken. Chop into small, bite-size pieces. Put the bamboo shoots, tofu, and chicken in a shallow saucepan with the dashi, soy sauce, and mirin. Bring to a boil over high heat. Reduce the heat to simmer for 15–20 minutes until all the cooking liquid has evaporated.

Put the sushi rice in a bowl, add the bamboo mixture, and stir to incorporate. Divide and transfer the sushi mixture to two serving dishes. Sprinkle with the nori, top with the sushi ginger, and serve with chopsticks.

Smoked salmon sushi

Serves 2

- 1/2 white or red onion, finely sliced
- 1 1/4 cups prepared sushi rice (page 132)
- juice of 1 lime
- 2 tablespoons capers, finely chopped
- 2 ounces smoked salmon, roughly chopped
- 2 big handfuls of arugula leaves
- 2 tablespoons salmon roe, mixed with 1 tablespoon sake
- 1 sheet of nori, torn into small pieces

Sushi is such a delicious, light food—perfect for supper—and this colorful dish will make you forget you're on a diet.

Start by soaking the onion slices in a bowl of cold water for 10 minutes (soaking rids the onion of the antisocial smell but retains the taste and crunchy texture) and drain.

Put the sushi rice in a bowl, sprinkle with the lime juice, and mix with the capers.

Divide and transfer the rice to two serving plates and arrange the smoked salmon pieces and arugula leaves on top. Scatter the onion over, and spoon the salmon roe on top. Garnish with the nori pieces and serve with chopsticks.

Marinated tuna sushi

This regional dish from Mie prefecture (southeast of Nagoya) derives its Japanese name, tekone zushi, from the fact that the soy-marinated tuna is mixed with the sushi rice by hand. It is a very satisfying and tactile way to prepare sushi.

Put the tuna in a bowl with all the ingredients for the soy marinade and leave for 30 minutes. Remove the tuna from the marinade and pat it dry.

Put the prepared sushi rice in a flat-based basin and add the marinated tuna, arugula leaves, scallion, and watercress.

With your hands, mix the rice with the tuna and greens to incorporate evenly. (Or if you prefer you can leave the rice and tuna unmixed and serve as picture opposite.)

Divide and transfer the sushi mixture to two serving dishes. Sprinkle with the sesame seeds, garnish with the shredded nori, and serve with chopsticks.

Serves 2

- 3$^1/_2$ ounces tuna steak, diced
- 1$^1/_4$ cups prepared sushi rice (page 132)
- a handful of arugula leaves, roughly chopped
- 1 scallion, finely chopped
- a handful of watercress
- 2 tablespoons toasted sesame seeds
- a handful of shredded nori

For the soy marinade
- 1 tablespoon toasted sesame seeds
- 1 scallion, finely chopped
- 2 tablespoons soy sauce
- 1 tablespoon sake
- 2 teaspoons wasabi paste

Lump crabmeat & pomegranate sushi

The pomegranate is called the "fruity panacea" because of its antioxidant properties. It may help to protect the body from heart disease, premature aging, Alzheimer's disease, and cancer. The fruit originates in Persia and has been the subject of myths and works of art. In this stunningly beautiful and refreshing recipe, both the ruby-like fruit and the juice are used.

Serves 2

- $^2/_3$ cup frozen fava beans
- $1^1/_4$ cups prepared sushi rice (page 132)
- seeds of 1 pomegranate
- $3^1/_4$ ounces lump crabmeat
- 2 tablespoons fresh cilantro, finely chopped
- 1 tablespoon fresh mint, finely chopped (optional)
- 1 tablespoon toasted sesame seeds

For the vinegar mix
- 2 tablespoons red wine vinegar
- 2 tablespoons pomegranate juice

Cook the fava beans in boiling water for 3 minutes, drain, and peel off the outer skin. (It is fiddly, but the result is well worth the extra effort.) Mix together the red wine vinegar and pomegranate juice for the vinegar mix.

Put the sushi rice in a mixing bowl, add the pomegranate, fava beans, and crabmeat. Pour the vinegar mix over the rice mixture, and with a sideways cutting motion, toss the rice to incorporate.

Divide the sushi mixture between two serving dishes, garnish with the cilantro and mint, and sprinkle with the sesame seeds. Serve with chopsticks.

Country-style kayu with chicken & miso

Serves 2

- 6 tablespoons Japanese short-grain rice
- 2 small boneless, skinless chicken thighs, trimmed and chopped into bite-size pieces
- 1 tablespoon sake
- 1 carrot, scrubbed clean
- 1 leek, trimmed
- ½ tablespoon sesame oil
- ½ cup frozen burdock
- 2½ cups Dashi (page 106)—secondary or water
- 2 shiitake mushrooms, stems discarded and caps sliced
- 4 snow peas, halved diagonally
- 4 tablespoon medium-colored miso paste
- 2 scallions, finely chopped diagonally
- 1 teaspoon toasted sesame seeds

Kayu is the Japanese word for rice porridge. Its origin is believed to go back to the confines of a solemn Zen Buddhist temple where monks started their long, Spartan training days with a bowl of plain rice porridge and a few slices of pickles. The monks' breakfast, however, makes a perfect light supper. There are a few types of kayu, all defined by the ratio of liquid to rice. For a dieter's evening meal, I recommend the "seven-portion kayu," which uses a ratio of seven portions of liquid to one portion of rice. This is a robust kayu, full of tastes and flavors that are guaranteed to leave you feeling satisfied and uplifted.

Wash and rinse the rice under cold, running water until the water runs clear and then set aside in a sieve to drain for at least 30 minutes. Put the chicken in a bowl and sprinkle with the sake.

Halve both the carrot and the leek lengthwise and then slice them diagonally. Place a wok over medium heat and add the sesame oil. When the wok is almost smoking hot, add the chicken and stir-fry for 3 minutes. Add the rice, burdock, carrot, and leek and stir-fry for 2–3 minutes before pouring in the dashi. Let the dashi come to a boil, reduce the heat to medium-low, cover the wok with a lid, and cook for 20 minutes.

Add the mushrooms and snow peas to the wok. Stir and cook for another 5 minutes. Put the miso paste in a big cooking ladle and submerge it in the rice to soften and dilute, then stir it in.

Add the scallions and gently stir to incorporate all the ingredients in the wok before turning off the heat. Divide and spoon into two bowls, sprinkle the sesame seeds on top, and serve immediately with chopsticks.

Dried shiitake mushroom kayu with spinach

This is an adaptation of a recipe originating in traditional Chinese medicine, in which a wide variety of dried mushrooms are used to boost the immune system. But you certainly don't have to be ill to enjoy this soothing yet satisfying kayu.

Wash and rinse the rice under cold, running water and set aside to drain in a sieve for at least 30 minutes. At the same time, put the shiitake mushrooms in a bowl and cover with enough boiling water to soften.

Sprinkle the sesame oil over the rice and toss to coat before placing it in a heavy-bottom saucepan with the dashi. Drain the shiitake mushrooms, reserving the soaking liquid, then slice the mushrooms and add them to the rice with the soaking liquid. Place the saucepan over high heat to bring to a boil, then reduce the heat to medium-low and simmer for 25–30 minutes.

Season with the soy sauce and mirin. Add the spinach and stir to soften before turning off the heat. Divide and ladle into two warm bowls, garnish with the scallion, sprinkle with the sesame seeds, and serve with chopsticks.

Serves 2

- 6 tablespoons Japanese short-grain rice
- 4 dried shiitake mushrooms caps
- $1/2$ tablespoon sesame oil
- $2^1/3$ cups Dashi (page 106)—secondary, water, or vegetarian
- 2 tablespoons soy sauce
- 1 tablespoon mirin
- 2 cups spinach, cleaned and roughly chopped
- 1 scallion, finely chopped diagonally
- 1 teaspoon toasted sesame seeds

Wakame kayu with miso & shimeji mushrooms

I am sure that you won't be surprised to hear that there are literally countless ways of cooking and seasoning rice in Japanese cuisine. This is a healthy and tasty combination of seaweeds, mushrooms, and miso paste that is sure to give you a comforting evening meal.

Wash and rinse the rice under cold, running water until the water runs clear. Set aside in a sieve to drain for at least 30 minutes. Put the rice in a heavy-bottom saucepan with the dashi and bring to a boil, covered, over high heat. When the rice reaches a boil and begins to boil over, lower the heat to simmer for 20 minutes.

Discard the base of the shimeji mushrooms and separate. Drain the wakame and add it to the rice with the carrot and shimeji. Continue to simmer for 10 minutes. Add the scallion.

Put the miso paste in a ladle and submerge into the rice to soften and dilute, and stir to incorporate. Turn off the heat, ladle into two warm bowls and serve immediately with chopsticks.

Serves 2

- 6 tablespoons Japanese short-grain rice
- $2^1/3$ cups Dashi (page 106)
- 1 pack (about 4 ounces) of shimeji mushrooms
- 1 tablespoon dried wakame, soaked in water to soften
- $1/2$ carrot, scrubbed clean and sliced diagonally
- 1 scallion, finely chopped
- 2 tablespoons medium-colored miso paste

Lump crabmeat kayu

Serves 2

- 6 tablespoons Japanese short-grain rice
- 7 ounces crabmeat in shell
- 1½ cups chopped napa cabbage
- 2½ cups Dashi (page 106)—secondary or water
- 2 tablespoons sake
- ½ teaspoon salt
- 2 tablespoons light soy sauce
- 1 egg, lightly beaten
- 2 scallions, finely chopped diagonally

When you manage to find crabmeat that is still in the shell, try this delicate but tasty kayu.

Wash and rinse the rice under cold, running water until the water runs clear and set aside in a sieve to drain for at least 30 minutes. Meanwhile, shell the crab and pick out the crabmeat. Put the rice, crab shells, and napa cabbage, along with the dashi, in a heavy-bottom saucepan and bring to a boil over high heat.

When it is boiling and begins to boil over, reduce the heat to medium-low and cook for 25–30 minutes. Discard the crab shells and add the crabmeat. Season with the sake, salt, and soy sauce and let it return to a boil.

Pour in the egg and stir to swirl. Turn off the heat when the egg begins to set. Ladle into two warm bowls, garnish with the scallions, and serve immediately with chopsticks

Shrimp & egg kayu

Serves 2

- 6 tablespoons Japanese short-grain rice
- 3½ ounces frozen shrimp
- 2⅓ cups Dashi (page 106)—secondary or water
- 1½ tablespoons light soy sauce
- 1½ tablespoons sake
- 2 eggs, lightly beaten
- a few sprigs of cilantro, roughly torn

I believe everyone should have a few tasty recipes that can quickly be rustled up with what's in the fridge—and this is one of them.

Wash and rinse the rice under cold, running water until the water runs clear and set aside in a sieve to drain for at least 30 minutes.

Put the rice in a heavy-bottom saucepan with the shrimp, dashi, soy sauce, and sake. Place the saucepan over a high heat to bring to the boil. Reduce the heat to low to simmer for 20 minutes.

Pour in the eggs and stir to swirl. Cook for 3 more minutes before turning off the heat. Divide and spoon into two warm bowls, garnish with the cilantro and serve immediately with chopsticks.

Oyster kayu

Serves 2

- 6 tablespoons Japanese short-grain rice
- 10 fresh oysters, shelled
- 2$\frac{1}{3}$ cups Dashi (page 106)—secondary, anchovy, or water
- $\frac{1}{2}$ teaspoon salt
- 1 tablespoon light soy sauce
- 1 teaspoon grated ginger
- zest of $\frac{1}{2}$ lemon, thinly sliced
- a few sprigs of cilantro, roughly torn
- 1 sheet of nori, crushed into small pieces
- 1 scallion, finely sliced

Kayu is very easy to digest and the ultimate comfort food, and with the addition of some fresh oysters you can make your supper a little bit more glamorous! I have two different garnish options for this recipe, either with lemon peel, cilantro, and nori, or simply with some scallions. It's up to you!

Start by washing and rinsing the rice until the water runs clear and set aside in a sieve to drain for at least 30 minutes. Put the oysters in a sieve and briefly rinse under cold, running water. Set aside to drain.

Put the rice, dashi, salt, and soy sauce in a heavy-bottom cast-iron saucepan with a tight-fitting lid. Bring to a boil over high heat and cook for 5 minutes. When it begins to boil over, adjust the lid and reduce the heat to medium-low to cook for 25–30 minutes.

Add the oysters, stir, and let the rice return to a boil. Stir in the grated ginger before turning off the heat. Divide and ladle into two warm bowls. Garnish with the slices of lemon zest, the cilantro, and crushed nori or, for a simpler approach, some scallion. Serve immediately with chopsticks.

Sea bream on rice

Serves 2

- 2 cups Japanese short-grain rice
- 5 ounces sea bream fillet
- $^1/_2$ teaspoon salt
- $1^1/_2$ cups Dashi (page 106)—primary or water
- 2 tablespoons + 1 teaspoon light soy sauce
- 2 tablespoons + 1 teaspoon sake
- a handful of cress

With its delicious taste, texture and appearance, sea bream is regarded as the King of Fish in Japan. No auspicious feast is complete without this handsome fish. It has well-balanced, high-quality protein and is easy to digest. If you can't find sea bream, substitute with red snapper.

Wash and rinse the rice under cold, running water until the water runs clear, and set aside in a sieve to drain for at least 30 minutes.

Meanwhile, preheat the broiler and cut the fish diagonally into bite-size slices $^1/_2$ inch thick. Sprinkle with the salt and set aside for 10 minutes. Broil the fish for 2 minutes on each side.

Put the rice in a heavy-bottom, shallow sauté pan with a solid lid. Add the dashi, soy sauce, and sake. Cover with the lid and bring to a boil over medium heat. Cook for 10 minutes or until the surface is free of the cooking liquid.

Spread the fish on top and cook for 5 minutes longer. Turn off the heat and let it steam for 10 minutes, before garnishing with the cress. Serve with chopsticks.

Three bean rice soup

Serves 2

- 1¼ cups Japanese-style short grain rice
- ¼ cup medium-grain rice
- 1¼ cups water
- ½ postcard-size piece of konbu
- scant ¼ cup shelled edamame
- scant ¼ cup shelled fava beans
- scant ¼ cup green peas
- 2 tablespoons sake
- ½ teaspoon salt
- 1 teaspoon toasted black sesame seeds

You may choose any combination of beans but this recipe is delicious with edamame, green peas, and fava beans, which, usefully, are all now available frozen.

Start by rinsing both types of rice until the water runs clear. Put them in a heavy-bottom saucepan with a tight-fitting lid. Add the measured amount of water along with the konbu and cook over low heat for 30 minutes.

Add the edamame, fava beans, peas, sake, and salt. Replace the lid and bring to a boil over low heat. Look out for signs that it has started to boil, such as bubbling sounds or thin ribbons of steam escaping from the pan, but do not lift up the lid to have a look.

Turn the heat up to high to cook for 3 minutes and then turn off the heat. Let it steam for 10 minutes before giving it a few stirs to fluff up the rice. Divide into two bowls, sprinkle the black sesame seeds on top, and serve with chopsticks.

Okonomiyaki (Japanese savory pancake)

Serves 2

- 2³/₄ cups finely shredded Savoy cabbage
- 1 cup bean sprouts, trimmed
- 2 scallions, finely chopped
- 1-inch piece of ginger, grated
- 4 tablespoons all-purpose flour
- ¹/₂ teaspoon salt
- 2 eggs
- 1 tablespoon vegetable oil
- 4 slices of streaky bacon, roughly chopped in bite-size pieces
- 2 handfuls of dried bonito fish flakes
- 2 tablespoons Japanese okonomiyaki sauce (or brown sauce)
- 2 tablespoons shredded nori

Okonomiyaki is a popular snack that dates back three hundred years to the streets of Tokyo. The main ingredients are shredded cabbage, eggs, and seasoned flour, which acts as a binding agent. Cook it like a pancake on a griddle or in an omelet pan.

Put the cabbage, bean sprouts, scallions, grated ginger, flour, salt, and eggs in a big bowl. Use a tablespoon to mix lightly, in cut-and-turn motions. Do not overmix, as it will make the mixture sticky and heavy.

Place an omelet pan over medium heat and add half of the oil. Pour half of the cabbage mixture into the pan. Sprinkle over half of the bacon and put a handful of bonito fish flakes on top—there's no need to press them down.

Cook for 5–6 minutes, then turn it over to cook the other side for 6–7 minutes, then turn it over again to cook for 3 minutes. Remove from the heat and keep warm while cooking the second half of the cabbage mixture in the same way.

Transfer the cooked okonomiyaki to two plates and spread with the Japanese okonomiyaki sauce using the back of a spoon. Sprinkle with the shredded nori and serve with chopsticks.

Zucchini okonomiyaki with tuna

Serves 2

- 4 zucchini, trimmed
- 1 red bell pepper, seeded and finely sliced
- 1 red onion, finely sliced
- a big handful of flat-leaf parsley, finely chopped
- 2 garlic cloves, grated
- 6 ounces canned tuna, drained and flaked
- 4 tablespoons all-purpose flour
- 1 teaspoon chile flakes
- 1/2 teaspoon salt
- 2 eggs
- 1 tablespoon vegetable oil
- a handful of dried bonito fish flakes

I created this version of the classic okonomiyaki one summer when there seemed to be no end of zucchini growing in my vegetable garden.

With a Japanese mandolin or grater, shred the zucchini, squeeze out the excess liquid, and fluff up. In a big bowl, combine all the ingredients except the oil and bonito fish flakes. Mix and incorporate in a cut-and-turn motion but do not overmix or the mixture will become too sticky and heavy.

Heat half of the oil in a frying pan over medium heat. Divide the zucchini mixture into two portions. Put one portion on the pan and gently spread the mixture to the size of a dessert plate size but do not press down.

Cook one side for 6–7 minutes, then turn over to cook the other side for 5–6 minutes. Repeat the process to cook the other half of the zucchini mixture. Transfer the okonomiyaki to a serving plate, garnish with bonito fish flakes, and serve with chopsticks.

Salmon hotpot

Hotpot is a great Japanese classic — family and friends sit around a big pot on the table, cooking seasonal or regional favourites. I have adapted it to make a healthy and tasty light supper that is easy to prepare by even the most reluctant cook.

Serves 2

- 4 tablespoons dried seaweed mix
- 1/2 large daikon radish, scrubbed clean
- 1 carrot, scrubbed clean
- 2 cups Dashi (page 106)
- 1 leek, trimmed and thinly sliced diagonally
- 1 1/2 cups thinly sliced napa cabbage
- 1 garlic clove, grated
- 3 1/2 ounces salmon fillet, sliced diagonally into bite-size pieces
- 4 tablespoons medium-colored or red miso paste
- 1 tablespoon lemon juice

Start by putting the seaweed mix in a bowl, cover with water, and set aside to soften. Cut the daikon into 1/3-inch thick slices and quarter each slice. Chop the carrot into 1/3-inch thick slices diagonally. Put the daikon and carrot in a saucepan with the dashi and bring to a boil over medium heat.

Drain the seaweed mix, and when the dashi begins to boil, reduce the heat and add the seaweed, leek, napa cabbage, garlic, and salmon. Cook for 10 minutes. Put the miso paste in a small bowl and ladle in a small amount of the dashi to dilute the paste. Add to the saucepan. Increase the heat to let the dashi return to a boil for 1 second. Ladle into two warm bowls, drizzle with the lemon juice, and serve with chopsticks.

Tofu hotpot

Tofu should not be cooked for a long time—it will develop small holes and become spongy. Think of warming the tofu rather than cooking it.

Serves 2

- 1 postcard-size piece of konbu
- 1 2/3 cups water
- 1/2 (12-ounce) package soft silken tofu
- soy sauce
- a handful of dried bonito fish flakes
- a handful of finely chopped scallions

Place the konbu in a saucepan, cover with the water, and let infuse for 30 minutes.

Cut the tofu into 1-inch cubes. Place the saucepan over low heat and bring to a boil slowly. When small bubbles begin to appear, add the tofu to heat gently until the tofu cubes start to shake in the water. Turn off the heat and divide between two warm dishes. Serve with soy sauce, bonito fish flakes, and scallions.

Warm salad of steamed plaice with creamy yofu dressing

Plaice is another dieters' dream fish—it is rich in high-quality protein, and low in fat and calories. It is also high in vitamin B1 and B2, which help to calm stresses, and its rich vitamin D helps the absorption of calcium and prevents osteoporosis. Its delicately flavored white flesh contains collagen that helps to maintain youthful skin. The best season for plaice is during the cold months and early spring—so having it in a warm salad is a perfect way to enjoy this wonderful fish.

You need 2 bamboo steaming baskets for this recipe. Cut the fish into manageable bite-size pieces. Put it in a shallow dish that fits into the bamboo steaming basket, and pour in the sake, and season with salt and pepper.

Cut the broccoli into bite-size pieces. Discard the lower parts of the asparagus and cut the spears into half lengths.

Put the fish dish in a bamboo basket with the lid on and place it over a saucepan with boiling water to steam over medium heat for 10–12 minutes.

Mix all the ingredients for the creamy yofu dressing while the fish is steaming.

Put the green beans in another basket, leaving enough room for the other vegetables, and put the basket underneath the fish basket. Continue to steam for 2 minutes, before adding all the other vegetables to steam for another 2 minutes.

Divide all the ingredients into two equal portions and arrange them on two serving dishes. Pour the dressing over each dish and serve with chopsticks.

Serves 2

- 7 ounces plaice fillet
- 4 tablespoons sake
- salt and freshly ground black pepper
- 7 ounces purple sprouting broccoli
- 6 asparagus spears
- 4 heaping tablespoons shelled fava beans
- 10 thin green beans, trimmed

For the creamy yofu dressing
- 4 tablespoons toasted sesame seeds, ground
- 6 tablespoons yofu (tofu yogurt)
- 1 tablespoon runny honey
- 2 tablespoons soy sauce
- 1/2 teaspoon sesame oil

Japanese rolled cabbage

Serves 2

- ½ head napa cabbage
- 7 ounces lean ground pork
- ½ onion, finely minced
- ½ carrot, finely minced
- 1 teaspoon grated ginger
- 1 egg yolk
- ½ teaspoon salt and pepper
- 3 teaspoons cornstarch
- 1 cup dashi (page 106)
- 2 tablespoons soy sauce
- 2 teaspoons cornstarch
- 4 teaspoons water
- a few mint leaves, very finely shredded

I used to be and still am somewhat averse to using the microwave oven, so it stood as one of the most underused items in my kitchen. But I am beginning to think again. Microwave cooking is quick, clean, and simple, especially when you are cooking a small quantity. This recipe makes full use of the microwave, but if you either don't have one or are adamantly against it, use a shallow sauté pan with a tight-fitting lid instead.

Cut the cabbage in half lengthwise—you should now have two quarters. Trim out the hard core but keep the cabbage joint at the base.

Mix the pork with the onion, carrot, ginger, egg yolk, salt and pepper, and 1 teaspoon of the cornstarch and divide into two equal portions.

With the back of a small spoon, spread the pork mixture in between the leaves and tie the cabbage with cooking string. Put the tied cabbage quarters on a microwave-proof dish that is large and deep enough to add the dashi later, cover with plastic wrap, prick the plastic wrap, and microwave for 8 minutes. Take the cabbages out of the dish and set aside. When the cabbages are cool enough to handle, remove the string, cut them into manageable-size pieces, and arrange them on serving dishes.

Mix the remaining 2 teaspoons cornstarch with the water. Add the dashi, soy sauce, and the cornstarch mixture to the dish and microwave for 2–3 minutes. Pour the mixture over the cabbages, garnish with the mint leaves, and serve.

Okay, so you're feeling peckish. That doesn't surprise me—you're on a diet, after all. But I urge you to persevere with *The Chopsticks Diet* because I know that you have nearly reached the goal you set yourself. Here are five recipes that got me through those dark moments when I was feeling hungry and tempted to grab whatever was available. My advice is to make one or two of the recipes when you have spare time, so that you can enjoy some guilt-free, low-calorie healthy snacks to fall back on even when you're busy.

Hunger busters

Spicy konnyaku cubes

Serves 2

- 1 (9-ounce) block konnyaku
- 1 teaspoon sesame oil
- 3 tablespoons soy sauce
- 1 tablespoon mirin
- ½ teaspoon chile flakes

Konnyaku is a dieter's dream food (see page 122 for its nutritional benefits). I make a large batch of these spicy cubes and nibble them over a few days whenever I feel peckish.

With your hands, tear the konnyaku into bite-size cubes. Bring a saucepan of water to a boil and poach the konnyaku cubes for 2–3 minutes. Drain and pat dry with paper towels.

Place a wok over high heat, add the oil, and stir-fry the konnyaku for 5 minutes.

Reduce the heat to medium, season with the soy sauce and mirin, and continue to cook until almost all the cooking liquid is gone.

Sprinkle with the chile flakes and transfer to a lidded container to store.

Tip
Don't worry about an uneven, jagged edge on the konnyaku cubes when you prepare them—this increases the surface area and therefore the flavor.

Kiriboshi daikon instant pickles

Serves 2

- 1½ ounces kiriboshi daikon
- 1 deep-fried tofu
- ½ tablespoon sesame oil
- ½ cup Dashi (page 106)
- 1 teaspoon sugar
- 1 tablespoon mirin
- 2 tablespoons soy sauce

Kiriboshi daikon is dried daikon that is rich in various minerals such as natrium, kalium, and calcium. It also contains high levels of edible fiber, but above all, it has a deep and comforting sweet taste.

Put the kiriboshi daikon in a large bowl of cold water and rub together to untangle the shreds. Drain and let stand for 5 minutes to soften before poaching in boiling water for 1 minute. Drain and when cool enough to handle, chop into manageable-size lengths.

Pour boiling water over the deep-fried tofu to rid it of excess oil. Cut the tofu in half lengthwise and cut into small strips.

Heat the oil in a shallow saucepan over high heat add the kiriboshi daikon and toss to coat, then add the tofu. Add the dashi, sugar, mirin, and soy sauce, then lower the heat to continue cooking while stirring with a pair of cooking chopsticks until almost all the cooking liquid is gone. Let it cool down before transferring into a lidded dish and eat within 3 days.

Crunchy rice crisps

Serves 2

- ⅓ cup leftover prepared sushi rice (page 132)
- 1 tablespoon toasted black sesame seeds

I have struggled for years to come up with a recipe for leftover sushi rice . . . and now I proudly present this to you to enjoy.

Preheat the oven to 160°C/325°F/Gas Mark 3. Mix the prepared sushi rice with the sesame seeds and spread on a large sheet of baking parchment.

Cover wtih another sheet of parchment and roll the rice out to a thin sheet with a rolling pin. Peel off the top parchment. Place the rice and bottom sheet in the oven and bake for 10–12 minutes or until it becomes dry and crisp, and browned on the outer edge.

Let it cool down completely, then peel the rice sheet off the parchment and break into rice crisps. Eat the same day.

Tomato jelly

- ¾ cup + 1 tablespoon tomato juice
- ½ teaspoon agar agar powder
- 1 teaspoon shredded nori
- a drizzle of balsamic vinegar (optional)

Here is another use of agar agar to create a healthy and stunning-looking jelly that you can snack on without guilt.

Put the tomato juice in a saucepan with the agar agar powder. Bring to a boil over medium heat. Once it starts to boil, reduce the heat to low and cook for 2 minutes.

Turn off the heat, pour it into a mold, and let it cool to room temperature before placing it in the fridge to set. Take the jelly out of the mold and cut into bite-size cubes. Eat within 2 days.

The tomato jelly is particularly nice to eat with a drizzle of vintage balsamic vinegar.

Green tea & soymilk jelly

- ¾ cup + 1 tablespoon soymilk
- ½ teaspoon agar agar powder
- 1 teaspoon fruit sugar or sugar
- 1 teaspoon matcha (green tea powder), mixed with 1 tablespoon hot water

Here is a tasty combination of three wonderful diet-friendly foods: green tea, soymilk, and agar agar.

Put the soymilk and agar agar in a saucepan and bring to a boil. Cook for 2–3 minutes. Add the sugar and dissolved green tea and stir to mix.

Turn off the heat, pour the mixture into a mold, and let it cool to room temperature before placing it in the fridge to set.

When it is set, cut into bite-size cubes and eat within 2 days.

Unlike in Western cuisine, where a sweet-flavored dessert is served at the end of a meal, Japanese cooking does not have desserts after dinner. Instead, a traditional Japanese meal will end on a savory note with a bowl of rice, served with a bowl of miso soup and a few slices of pickled vegetables. Once the table has been cleared, seasonal fruits may be served along with some cleansing green tea, but these are strictly for "after the meal." The Japanese, especially women and children, do love their sweets and desserts, but traditional Japanese confectioneries are enjoyed between meals, and most often in the middle of the afternoon with tea.

The health and aesthetic benefits of green teas are widely recognized; catechin, which gives the distinctive astringent taste, is an antioxidant known to slow down the ageing process; it also lowers cholesterol and blood pressure, and combined with its high vitamin C content, it is very good for skin. But much of the beneficial element is non-aqueous and so to get the full advantage you need to "eat" rather than drink the tea. The practice of eating teas has long existed in China and in Japan, in the form of tea ceremonies where green tea powder is used. I have created a few green tea–themed desserts (along with other low-fat suggestions) to give you guilt-free sweetness to round off your meals.

Desserts

Crème green tea

Serves 2

- 2 teaspoons toasted sesame seeds
- 2 teaspoons matcha
- 2 tablespoons brown sugar
- ½ teaspoon agar agar powder
- ¾ cup + 1 tablespoon soymilk
- 2 raspberries

In this recipe, green tea, agar agar, and soymilk are brought together to create a delicious, healthy, guilt-free dessert. Agar agar is a type of seaweed that is not dissimilar to gelatin but is vegetarian and has a much greater ability to set. It has no calories, is rich in minerals, notably iron and calcium, and has an incredible amount of edible fiber so it leaves you feeling satisfied for a long time. Agar agar is also known to help to lower cholesterol, blood pressure, and body fat; altogether it is an ideal ingredient for healthy weight loss.

Put the sesame seeds in a mortar and grind with a pestle until smooth. Add the matcha and brown sugar and continue to grind until the mixture becomes uniform and smooth.

Dissolve the agar agar in a little bowl with 1 tablespoon of the soymilk. In a heatproof bowl, mix the rest of the soymilk with the tea mixture and add the agar agar. Cover the bowl with a piece of plastic wrap and microwave for 90 seconds on medium, stirring occasionally.

Remove the plastic wrap and pour the mixture into two serving glasses. Let them cool to room temperature before refrigerating until set. Place a raspberry in the center of each glass and serve. (For three servings—see picture—multiply the quantities by a third.)

Watermelon cubes

Serves 2

- 14 ounces watermelon, skinned
- 2 tablespoons white sesame seeds
- 2 tablespoons black sesame seeds

This is a refreshing and delicious way to eat watermelon.

Deseed the watermelon. Cut into bite-size cubes.

Put the white and black sesame seeds on separate plates. Dip one side of the watermelon cubes into the seeds and serve with chopsticks.

Green tea sherbet

Serves 2

- ³/₄ cup water
- 3 tablespoons sugar
- 2 teaspoons matcha, mixed with 2 tablespoons hot water

Sherbet is the perfect ice-cream substitute for dieters.

Put the water and sugar in a saucepan to heat until all the sugar is dissolved. Add the dissolved matcha and mix well to incorporate. Pour into an ice cube tray.

When it has cooled to room temperature, put the tray in the freezer for 30 minutes or until the edges begin to ice.

With a fork, stir to fluff up the semi-ice and return to the freezer to continue freezing until firm.

Green tea hotcake

Serves 2

- ³/₄ cup self-rising flour
- ¹/₄ cup superfine sugar
- 1 teaspoon matcha (green tea powder)
- 1 egg, lightly beaten
- 2 tablespoons mirin
- 3 tablespoons water
- 1 teaspoon vegetable oil
- slices of seasonal fruit of your choice

This is an adaptation of the traditional Japanese confectionery called dorayaki. They are hotcakes, about the size of tennis balls, with sweet adzuki bean paste in the middle. It is great to serve with slices of your favorite fruit, either as a dessert or as a quick breakfast.

Sift the flour, sugar, and matcha into a bowl and make a well in the center. Add the beaten egg, mirin, and water. Mix together with a whisk.

Place a nonstick pan over low heat with the oil and ladle in half of the hotcake mixture. Cook for 2–3 minutes or until little holes begin to appear. Turn over the hotcake to cook the other side for 2–3 minutes. Repeat the process to cook the other half of the hotcake mixture. Serve with slices of fruit.

Green tea agar agar jelly with grapefruit

Serves 2

- ³/₄ cup plus 1 tablespoon water
- ¹/₂ teaspoon agar agar
- 1 teaspoon matcha (green tea powder)
- 2 tablespoons mirin
- 1 tablespoon superfine sugar
- 1 grapefruit

This is a stunningly beautiful chilled dessert that is also kind to your body and skin.

Put the water and agar agar in a saucepan. Bring to a boil over medium heat while stirring, and continue to cook and stir for 2 minutes, before turning off the heat.

Put the matcha in a small bowl, add the mirin, and mix well. Add the matcha mixture and the sugar to the mixture in the saucepan and stir well. Pour the mixture into a mold, let it cool to room temperature, and refrigerate to set for 10 minutes.

Meanwhile, peel and segment the grapefruit. With a dessertspoon, scoop the matcha jelly into two chilled glass dishes, arrange the grapefruit segments on top, and serve.

Index

A

Adzuki beans, 10
  adzuki & rice porridge, 20
Agar agar, 10
Arugula
  Japanese ceviche of plaice with grapefruit & arugula, 85
  nori & arugula soba in broth, 50
  seafood & arugula domburi, 37
  seared beef, arugula, & grapefruit with wasabi dressing, 100
Asparagus
  asparagus & anchovy domburi, 31
  asparagus, green beans & hijiki soba noodle salad, 74
  asparagus, pea & new potato miso soup with salmon, 125
Avocado
  daikon, edamame & avocado salad with yuzu vinaigrette, 79
  tofu, crabmeat & avocado salad with wasabi dressing, 80
  tuna, avocado & spinach salad with wasabi dressing, 95
Azuki, 10

B

Bamboo shoots, 15
  bamboo shoot sushi, 133
Beans
  asparagus, green beans & hijiki soba noodle salad, 74
  fava bean & crabmeat domburi, 37
  mixed beans & beansprouts with chile sesame soy dressing, 75
  potato, green bean, tomato, & spinach salad with minty soy dressing, 73
  smoked mackerel, broccoli, green bean salad with miso sesame dressing, 92
  three bean rice soup, 148
Beef
  beef carpaccio & eggplant with ginger dressing, 100
  seared beef, arugula, & grapefruit with wasabi dressing, 100
Blueberries
  steamed green tea & blueberry muffins, 22
Bonito fish flakes, 10, 13
Breakfast, traditional, 16
Broccoli
  eggplant & broccoli, 133
  smoked mackerel, broccoli, green bean salad with miso sesame dressing, 92
  soba noodles with pickled plums & sprouting broccoli, 46
  sobaghetti with broccoli, 57
  tofu, seaweed, leek, & sprouting broccoli miso soup, 119
Burdock, 10
  spinach & burdock miso soup with maitake mushrooms, 116
  country-style kayu with chicken & miso, 140

C

Cabbage
  Japanese rolled cabbage, 156
  quick-pickled spring cabbage with sweet vinaigrette, 76
  soba noodles with napa cabbage & tofu, 44
Chicken
  country-style kayu with chicken & miso, 140
  leek & turnip miso soup with chicken, 121
  leftover chicken, cucumber, & soba noodle salad with spicy miso & sesame dressing, 96
  shredded chicken salad with creamy tofu dressing, 99
  vegetable & chicken salad with sesame miso dressing, 99
Citron, Japanese, 15
Clam chowder miso soup with crispy deep-fried tofu, 126
Corn
  Japanese corn chowder, 117
Crab
  fava bean & crabmeat domburi, 37
  lump crabmeat & pomegranate sushi, 138
  lump crabmeat kayu, 143
  tofu, crabmeat, & avocado salad with wasabi dressing, 80

D

Daikon, 10
  baked eggplant with grated daikon on green tea soba noodles, 49
  classic salmon sashimi with daikon salad, 86
  daikon, edamame, & avocado salad with yuzu vinaigrette, 79
  kiriboshi daikon instant pickles, 162
  salmon roe & grated daikon soba noodles, 58
  scallop sashimi with daikon salad, 89
  smoked salmon, daikon, & cucumber salad with watercress dressing, 88
Dashi, 106, 107
Devil's tongue, 13
Domburi, 28
Duck, crisp with orange & watercress salad, 103

E

Edamame
  chilled miso soup of eggplant, tomato, edamame, & cucumber, 108
  daikon, edamame & avocado salad with yuzu vinaigrette, 79
Eggplant
  baked eggplant with grated daikon on green tea soba noodles, 49
  beef carpaccio & eggplant with ginger dressing, 100
  chilled miso soup of eggplant, tomato, edamame & cucumber, 108
  eggplant & broccoli sushi, 133
  grilled eggplant & sweet pepper salad with ginger mustard, 111
Eggs
  egg & spinach domburi, 32
  Japanese rolled omelet with nori, 25
  shrimp & egg kayu, 143
  swirled egg brown rice porridge, 21
  swirling egg soba noodles in broth, 56
  tofu Spanish omelet, 25

G

Gobou, 10
Goma, 10

H

Hijiki, 10
Horseradish, Japanese green, 15

J

Japanese rice porridge, 19
Japanese savoury pancake, 149

K

Katsua-bushi, 10
Kayu
  country-style kayu with chicken & miso, 140
  dried shiitake mushroom kayu with spinach, 142
  lump crabmeat kayu, 143
  oyster kayu, 144
  shrimp & egg kayu, 143
  wakame kayu with miso & shimeji mushrooms, 142
Kome, 13
Konbu, 13
Konnyaku, 13
  pork miso soup with konnyaku, 122
  spicy konnyaku cubes, 161
Konten, 10

L

Leeks
  leek & turnip miso soup with chicken, 121
  tofu, seaweed, leek, & sprouting broccoli

miso soup, 119
Lentils
  spiced lentils with shrimp, 38
  warm lentils with tofu & spinach, 40
Lotus root, 14
M
Mirin, 13
Miso, 13, 14
  asparagus, pea & new potato miso soup with salmon, 125
  caramelized onion miso soup with burnt tofu, 120
  chilled miso soup of eggplant, tomato, edamame, & cucumber, 108
  chilled misopacho, 110
  clam chowder miso soup with crispy deep-fried tofu, 126
  country-style kayu with chicken & miso, 142
  creamy roast pumpkin miso soup, 114
  grilled eggplant & sweet pepper salad with ginger mustard, 111
  Japanese corn chowder, 117
  Japanese mushroom miso soup, 113
  leek & turnip miso soup with chicken, 121
  pork miso soup with konnyaku, 122
  shrimp & tomato miso soup with okra,129
  soup, making, 107
  spinach & burdock miso soup with maitake mushrooms, 116
  stir-fry soybeans with spicy miso, 43
  tofu, seaweed, leek, & sprouting broccoli miso soup, 119
  wakame kayu with miso & shimeji mushrooms, 142
Muffins, steamed green tea & blueberry, 22
Mushrooms
  chile mushroom & tofu domburi, 34
  dried shiitake mushroom kayu with spinach, 142
  Japanese mushroom miso soup, 113
  Japanese mushrooms with soba noodles in green tea broth, 51
  spinach & burdock miso soup with maitake mushrooms, 116
  wakame kayu with miso & shimeji mushrooms, 142
N
Nori, 14
  Japanese rolled omelet with nori, 25
  nori & arugula soba in broth, 50
  omusubi, 67
O
Okonomiyaki, 149
  zucchini okonomiyaki with tuna, 150
Okra
  shrimp & tomato miso soup with okra,129
  tuna, tomato, & okra domburi, 38
Omusubi, 67
Oyster kayu, 144
P
Peas

asparagus, pea & new potato miso soup with salmon, 125
Plaice
  Japanese ceviche of plaice with grapefruit & arugula, 85
  warm salad of steamed plaice with creamy yofu dressing, 155
Plums
  pickled, 15
  soba noodles with pickled plums & sprouting broccoli, 46
Pork
  Japanese rolled cabbage, 156
  pork miso soup with konnyaku, 122
Porridge
  adzuki & rice porridge, 20
  Japanese rice porridge, 19
  swirled egg brown rice porridge, 21
Potatoes
  asparagus, pea, & new potato miso soup with salmon, 125
  potato, green bean, tomato, & spinach salad with minty soy dressing, 73
Pumpkin
  creamy roast pumpkin miso soup, 114
R
Radish, Japanese giant white. See Daikon
Rencon, 14
Rice, 13
  adzuki & rice porridge, 20
  asparagus & anchovy domburi, 31
  broad bean & crabmeat domburi, 37
  brown, cooking, 31
  chile mushroom & tofu domburi, 34
  crunchy rice crisps, 163
  egg & spinach domburi, 32
  Japanese rice porridge, 19
  kayu. See Kayu
  sea bream on rice, 147
  seafood & arugula domburi, 37
  sushi. See Sushi
  swirled egg brown rice porridge, 21
  three bean rice soup, 148
  tuna, tomato, & okra domburi, 38
  zucchini & tomato domburi, 32
S
Sake, 14
  mirin, 13
Salad, 70
  asparagus, green beans, & hijiki soba noodle salad, 74
  classic salmon sashimi with daikon salad, 86
  crisp duck with orange & watercress salad, 103
  daikon, edamame, & avocado salad with yuzu vinaigrette, 79
  leftover chicken, cucumber & soba noodle salad with miso & sesame dressing, 96
  potato, green bean, tomato, & spinach salad with minty soy dressing, 73
  salt salmon & noodle salad, 88

scallop sashimi with daikon salad, 89
  shredded chicken salad with creamy tofu dressing, 99
  shrimp & bell pepper salad with chile soy dressing, 94
  smoked mackerel, broccoli, green bean salad with miso sesame dressing, 92
  smoked salmon, daikon, & cucumber salad with watercress dressing, 88
  squid salad with soy vinegar dressing, 91
  tofu Caesar salad, 80
  tofu, crabmeat, & avocado salad with wasabi dressing, 80
  tofu salad, 82
  tuna, avocado, & spinach salad with wasabi dressing, 95
  vegetable & chicken salad with sesame miso dressing, 99
  warm salad of steamed plaice with creamy yofu dressing, 155
Salmon
  asparagus, pea, & new potato miso soup with salmon, 125
  classic salmon sashimi with daikon salad, 86
  salmon furikake (sprinkles), 65
  salmon hotpot, 152
  salmon roe & grated daikon soba noodles, 58
  salt salmon & noodle salad, 88
  smoked salmon, daikon & cucumber salad with watercress dressing, 88
  smoked salmon sushi, 134
Scallops
  scallop sashimi with daikon salad, 89
  seared scallops & soba noodles with mizuna pesto, 55
Sea bream on rice, 147
Seafood & arugula domburi, 37
Seaweed
  hijiki, 10
  Japanese rolled omelette with nori, 25
  kelp, 13
  nori, 14
  nori & arugula soba in broth, 50
  soft, 15
  tofu, seaweed, leek & sprouting broccoli miso soup, 119
Sesame seeds, 10
Shoyu, 14
Shrimps
  seafood & arugula domburi, 37
  shrimp & egg kayu, 143
  shrimp & bell pepper salad with chile soy dressing, 94
  shrimp & tomato miso soup with okra,129
  spiced lentils with shrimps, 38
Smoked mackerel, broccoli, green bean salad with miso sesame dressing, 92
Smoothies, 26
Soba noodles, 14

asparagus, green beans, & chili soba
   noodle salad, 74
baked eggplant with grated daikon on
   green tea soba noodles, 49
chilled soba noodles with gazpacho sauce,
   52
Japanese mushrooms with soba noodles in
   green tea broth, 51
leftover chicken, cucumber, & soba noodle
salad with spicy miso & sesame dressing, 96
nori & arugula soba in broth, 50
salmon roe & grated daikon soba noodles,
   58
salt salmon & noodle salad, 88
seared scallops & soba noodles with
   mizuna pesto, 55
soba noodles with napa cabbage &
   tofu, 44
soba noodles with pickled plums &
   sprouting broccoli, 46
sobaghetti with broccoli, 57
swirling egg soba noodles in broth, 56
wakame & spinach soba noodles with
   sesame dipping sauce, 45
Sobu, 14
Soups, 104
   miso. See Miso
   three bean rice soup, 148
Soy beans
   miso, 13, 14
   stir-fry soy beans with spicy miso, 43
   tofu, 15
Soy sauce, 14
Spinach
   dried shiitake mushroom kayu with
     spinach, 142
   egg & spinach domburi, 32
   potato, green bean, tomato & spinach
     salad with minty soy dressing, 73
   spinach & burdock miso soup with
     maitake mushrooms, 116
   tuna, avocado, & spinach salad with
     wasabi dressing, 95

wakame & spinach soba noodles with
   sesame dipping sauce, 45
warm lentils with tofu & spinach, 40
Spring rolls, fresh, 68
Squid
   seafood & arugula domburi, 37
   squid salad with soy vinegar dressing, 91
Su, 14, 15
Sushi
   bamboo shoot sushi, 133
   eggplant & broccoli, 133
   lump crabmeat & pomegranate sushi, 138
   marinated tuna sushi, 137
   rice, preparing, 132
   rolled sushi, 62
   smoked salmon sushi, 134
   stuffed sushi, 64
T
Takenoko, 15
Tea, 15
   crème green tea, 168
   green tea agar agar jelly with grapefruit,
     173
   green tea & soy milk jelly, 164
   green tea & tofu smoothie, 26
   green tea hotcake, 173
   green tea milkshake, 26
   green tea sherbet, 170
   steamed green tea & blueberry muffins, 22
Tofu, 15
   caramelized onion miso soup with burnt
     tofu, 120
   chile mushroom & tofu domburi, 34
   clam chowder miso soup with crispy deep-
     fried tofu, 126
   green tea & tofu smoothie, 26
   soba noodles with napa cabbage & tofu,
     44
   tofu & apple smoothie, 26
   tofu & strawberry smoothie, 26
   tofu Caesar salad, 80
   tofu, crabmeat, & avocado salad with
     wasabi dressing, 80

tofu hotpot, 152
tofu salad, 82
tofu, seaweed, leek, & sprouting broccoli
   miso soup, 119
tofu Spanish omelette, 25
warm lentils with tofu & spinach, 40
Tomatoes
   chilled miso soup of eggplant, tomato,
     edamame, & cucumber, 108
   chilled soba noodles with gazpacho sauce,
     52
   potato, green bean, tomato & spinach
     salad with minty soy dressing, 73
   shrimp & tomato miso soup with okra,
     129
   tomato jelly, 164
   tuna, tomato, & okra domburi, 38
   zucchini & tomato domburi, 32
Tuna
   marinated tuna sushi, 137
   tuna, avocado, & spinach salad with
     wasabi dressing, 95
   tuna, tomato & okra domburi, 38
   zucchini okonomiyaki with tuna, 150
U
Umeboshi, 15
V
Vinegar, 14, 15
W
Wakame kayu with miso & shimeji
   mushrooms, 142
Wakame, 15
   wakame & spinach soba noodles with
     sesame dipping sauce, 45
   wakame & green tea furikake, 65
Wasabi, 15
Watermelon cubes, 170
Y
Yuzu, 15
Z
Zucchini
   zucchini & tomato domburi, 32
   zucchini okonomiyaki with tuna, 150

Directory

Mitsuwa www.mitsuwa.com
Stores in California, Illinois, New Jersey.

H Mart and Super H Mart www.hmart.com
Stores in California, Colorado, Georgia, Illinois,
Maryland, New York, New Jersey, Oregon,
Pennsylvania, Texas, Virginia, Washington.

Uwajimaya www.uwajimaya.com
Stores in Washington and Oregon.

Ranch 99 www.ranch99.com
Stores in California, Georgia, Washington.
Hong Kong Food Market, 925 Behrman Highway
Terrytown, LA, 504-394-7075

Daruma Japan Market, 6931-E Arlington Road
Bethesda, MD, 301-654-8832

Kotobukiya, Inc. www.kotobukiyamarket.com
1815 Massachusetts Avenue
Cambridge, MA, 617-354-6914

One World Market, 42705 Grand River Avenue
Novi, MI, 248-374-0844

Katagiri & Co., Inc., 224 East 59th Street
New York, NY, 212-755-3566

Tensuke Market, 1167 Old Henderson Road
Columbus, OH, 614-451-6002

Nam Hai Oriental Food Market, 1924 S. Garnett
Road, Tulsa, OK, 918-438-0166